Who, Me, Give a Speech?

HANDBOOK
FOR CHRISTIAN WOMEN

Nancy T. Alford

BAKER BOOK HOUSE
Grand Rapids, Michigan 49516

Copyright 1987 by
Baker Book House Company

ISBN: 0-8010-0211-7

Printed in the United States of America

In memory of my mother,
Ida Seeley

Contents

PART 3: Polish

PART 4: Prime

PART 5: Proceed

Acknowledgments

I would like to express a sincere thank you to Delores Peckam for believing in me; to my family, John, Heather, and Casey, for putting up with me; to my mentors Don and Doris Mainprize who molded me into a writer; to Gala Muntz for typing all my scribbles and remaining positive; to the Reverend Eric Fenton for his guidance; and to all the people who supported me in prayer.

1

From Potlucks to Podiums
Are you ready?

Go into all the world and preach the gospel to all creation.
Mark 16:15

You approach the podium. Noisily your tongue peels itself from the roof of your mouth. You wonder where the saliva went until it pops out on your forehead and cascades down the side of your face. Mouth open, you find your mind blank, unable to recall that witty beginning line. Cold hands frantically fumble through note cards. A red flush hotly creeps across your face and neck. Knees trembling, stomach churning, your halting voice begins, "... ahhh ..."

Sound familiar? You are not alone. Daily, thousands of Christian women are called from church kitchens to speaker's platforms. Unequipped, inexperienced, and white knuckled,

11

they grip the podiums and serve in the public eye for the first time.

Most individuals are reluctant speakers beset by these symptoms of stage fright. A study of fifty thousand college students shows seventy percent experience great anxiety when speaking to a large audience. Percentages decrease with audience size, but still ten to fifteen percent are nervous when talking to only one person. Fear causes many never to reach the podium. Others do, but the audience must bear the cross of a speech beyond salvation.

In a college speech class an intelligent, casually dressed grandmother spoke on the importance of marital fidelity. Her face flashed terror as her eyes darted from notes to ceiling, bypassing the audience entirely. Unfortunately, her speech was not persuasive. Although Scripturally sound, her argument was poorly researched, poorly prepared, and delivered without enthusiasm. She clutched the podium and mumbled a barely audible speech. How unfortunate that this Christian message had all the appeal of an overstarched collar.

The following week a peppy young divorcee, dressed in a floor-length gown, retaliated in a dramatic rebuttal. The stage was set with low lights, soft music, a couch, and a table complete with flowers. Entered the fictitious boyfriend with a bottle of wine in his hand and a look of lust on his face. They snuggled on the couch while cooing and kissing. The class loved it. After this graphic demonstration the speaker enthusiastically recommended having an affair during a bad marriage (as she had done) in order to regain self-confidence.

Certainly the divorcee's reasoning was faulty, but her charm, skill, and creativity in communicating her point were first rate.

We need to free the expression of all that we are and

have in Christ. As Christians we must ignite spiritual fires within our listeners, fires that spread across the vast prairies of internal emptiness, burning out the old, releasing the new. If we don't, someone else will.

There is an army of articulate Antichrists talking hundred of thousands of innocent sheep into their folds. Need we be reminded of Madeline O'Hare, Jim Jones, and Rev. Sun Myung Moon? Like silver-tongued dragons, the world breathes lies and perversions with eloquence and skill. Should we Christians be less skilled in speaking truth?

Approximately five million speeches are given annually in the United States,[1] but according to professional speech writer Joseph J. Kelley, Jr., few are remembered. The many reasons Kelley gives fall into two categories: lack of effort and lack of skill. We expect speech preparation to go easily and overlook craftsmanship. Standing stonefaced and stiff, we speak of our faith in a monotone and expect unbelievers to be moved.

Paul said, "Be diligent to present yourself approved to God as a workman who does not need to be ashamed, handling accurately the word of truth" (2 Tim. 2:15). By this Paul means study and work. We need both to be able to represent God as worthy ambassadors. A commitment to Christ means you have made yourself available for his use. There is true joy in working toward his goals.

Is God moving in your life? Have you shared your faith with a friend over coffee? Are you a pastor's wife, lay leader, Sunday school teacher? Do you volunteer, belong to a club or committee? Have you expertise in a craft or skill? Are you a housewife, or do you work in the marketplace of the

---

1. Joseph J. Kelley, *Speechwriting: The Master Touch* (Harrisburg, Pa.: Stackpole, 1980),.p. 11.

secular world? If the answer is yes to any of these questions, you may be asked to speak.

As unbelievable as this may sound, God is calling women out of their "comfort zones" as Dr. Vonette Bright, cofounder of Campus Crusade for Christ, would put it. Mission fields are everywhere: in your home, in your neighborhood — even while you worship, the lost pass by on the sidewalk outside your church.

God's call to women is nothing new. He used women throughout the Bible as his representatives. God sent Abigail to David after her husband insulted him. A risky speech assignment. Her ego and her life were in danger. She carried to David God's affirmation that he would be mightily used. This persuasive speech changed Abigail's life.

Priscilla was a contemporary of Paul and leader in the church. She wasn't gossiping with the neighborhood women over donuts and coffee. She was busy in her home organizing the church at Ephesus. Not only that, she taught others, including the prominent Apollos who came to Ephesus to speak.[2]

The most critical message in the history of mankind God entrusted to a woman. She was Mary Magdalene, who delivered word of the risen Christ to the disciples. Imagine the convincing that was necessary and how inadequate Mary must have felt, especially when the disciples didn't believe her! What if she didn't like the job description and had failed to relay the good news?

When Moses was called to speak on God's behalf he hedged. "Please, Lord, I have never been eloquent, ... I am slow of speech and slow of tongue ..." (Exod. 4:10). Moses had good old-fashioned stage fright. Jeremiah also objected

2. Edith Deen, *All the Women of the Bible* (New York: Harper and Row, 1955), pp. 228–29.

when God called him. "Alas, LORD God! Behold I do not
know how to speak (Jer. 1:6). Although neither Moses nor
Jeremiah considered themselves talented speakers, God still
called them to this task.

Today we needlessly echo their reluctance. How unfortunate. Within each normal, average woman are the raw
materials of a public speaker. Yes, even you!

Knowing what to do helps. Moses and Jeremiah received
instruction directly from God. Within these pages you are
given the tools to discover God's message written in your
life and the speech framework into which it should be placed.
Even if you have already done some speaking, there is still
much to be learned about the craft.

We are not all called to a public-speaking ministry, but
as Christians we have a message to deliver. Everyone should
be able to make a one-minute announcement, introduce
someone properly, and give a three-minute testimony of her
faith.

Do you emphatically express yourself to your husband?
Can you reprimand your children with conviction? Do you
share prayer concerns with great fervor? Public speaking
does not take extraordinary talent. Its principles are the
same as simple conversation.[3] What it requires is a willing-
ness to learn the craft and serve an audience. If more people
were willing, the workers would not be so few (see Matt.
9:37).

We Christian women are powerful tools for Kingdom work.
There is a dying world weary of sin. There is a Christian
world weary of battle. How wonderful to be able to reach
others with articulated hope.

Whether speaking to one or one thousand, do you skill-
fully and enthusiastically represent Christ? Peter cautioned,

3. Charles R. Gruner, *Plain Public Speaking* (New York: Macmillan, 1983), p. 97.

"Sanctify Christ as Lord in your hearts, always *being* ready to make a defense to every one who asks you to give an account for the hope that is in you ..." (1 Peter 3:15).

Are you ready?

Work Sheet

1. Make a list of all the excuses you have for not being a public speaker.
2. Throw the list away and go on to the next chapter.

Part **1**

Prepare

2

Flying Your Butterflies in Formation

Understanding and overcoming stage fright

For I am the LORD your God, who upholds your right hand, Who says to you, 'Do not fear, I will help you.'

Isaiah 41:13

Laliophobia. Do you have this dreaded social problem? Ten million Americans suffer from excessive fears,[1] but this phobia consistently tops the list. A 1973 poll, the 1977 bestseller *The Book of Lists*, the Bruskin Report, and a 1983 survey all cite America's number one fear: public speaking. The fear of public speaking continues to outrank that of heights, snakes, and death. In other words, most

1. Judith A. Ermold, "Hope for Prisoners of Fear," ON *Magazine* (February 1983):34.

people would rather fall into a pit of snakes and die than give a speech.

Fear is no respecter of persons. The icy fingers of anxiety creep up the spines of amateur and professional alike.

I met a professional speaker quite by accident one evening at a conference. As we chatted I recognized her from a brochure. This charming lady spends several months each year traveling to various speaking engagements, besides being an editor, author, and wife.

"Aren't you tonight's speaker?" I inquired.

"Yes," she quickly responded. "I just flew in from Denver this morning, and I'm soooo nervous."

"I'm sure you'll do fine," I said encouragingly.

"You know," she continued as if not hearing me, "I shouldn't have eaten that taco for lunch. It made me so thirsty that I've been drinking water all afternoon. I'll probably have to go to the bathroom right in the middle of my speech! I can see it now." Then, deepening her voice and changing her facial expression, she added, "Excuse me, ladies and gentlemen, while I go to the restroom."

A delightful, but nervous lady. I was amazed at how openly she revealed her fear, especially after I heard her speak. She was outstanding!

Leo Buscaglia, another professional, describes his first lecture at the University of Southern California with such terms as "With a great deal of anxiety . . . I started my lecture stammering. . . . At that moment of panic. . . ."[2]

Doctors, too, experience panic when it comes to public speaking. One such doctor was a baseball fan and attended all his favorite team's games. Recognizing his loyalty, they invited him to a banquet.

2. Leo Buscaglia, "The Girl in the Fifth Row," *Reader's Digest* (February 1984):33, 34.

Suddenly, with the abruptness and unexpectedness of an explosion, he heard the toastmaster remark: "We have a physician with us tonight, and I am going to ask Dr. Curtis to talk on a Baseball Player's Health."

Was he prepared? Of course. He had had the best preparation in the world: he had been studying hygiene and practicing medicine for almost a third of a century. . . .

He was in positive misery. He knew that if he got up he would fail, that he would be unable to utter half a dozen sentences. So he arose, and without saying a word, turned his back on his friends and walked silently out of the room, a deeply embarrassed and humiliated man.[3]

As a professional speaker, Erma Bombeck recognizes this problem. She suggests, "Demand a podium capable of supporting a dead body (yours) up to 187 pounds. Throw yourself over it, being sure to hook your arm over the microphone so you won't slip away."[4] There are other solutions to this problem.

First, fear needs to be understood before it can be controlled. It operates on a mental and spiritual plane, but manifests itself physically. Author and professional speaker Charles R. Gruner says our autonomic nervous system is to blame for our physical responses. Our ancestors were instilled with a healthy fear response to the dangers of primitive living. With wild animals at every turn of the path, the body adapted to fight or flight. Our bodies respond to speech giving as if to a confrontation with a prehistoric predator. Bodily changes result, causing cold extremities, shortness of breath, shaking, and various digestive disorders.

Actually, our self-image, not our life, is in danger. Gruner

3. Dale Carnegie, *How to Develop Self-Confidence and Influence People by Public Speaking* (New York: Pocket Books, 1956), p. 3.
4. Erma Bombeck, "A practiced public speaker has nothing (much) to fear."

identifies six self-images that are threatened when we speak: intellectual, social, sexual, professional, cosmetic, and economic.[5] This means we want the audience to think, "My, what an attractive, feminine, brilliant speaker. I like her. Let's pass the plate."

To the Christian speaker I would also like to suggest that we are concerned with our spiritual self-images, and rightly so. After all, this is most crucial. Our relationship with God should be a deep and ever-abiding one. This must be projected to the audience in order to win their trust.

We fear negative opinions. This concern causes our physical undoing. So we must ride roughshod over our feelings and hogtie fear before it defeats us.

The Bible commands almost 90 times to "fear not." Sometimes this command is coupled with the phrase "neither be dismayed." Dismay is from a Hebrew word that means to break down from confusion and fear. Satan wins when we allow fear to trample our abilities.

Fear is the biggest obstacle to overcome in public communication. This negative emotion muzzles many a would-be speaker. Fear keeps us from sharing our faith. Fear keeps us from serving in Sunday school. Fear keeps us from helping others find eternal life. We forget it is a spirit not from God. He gave us love, power, and a sound mind (see 2 Tim. 1:7). It's God's opinion that counts. The audience is not a pack of saber-toothed tigers. Remember, he who is in you is greater than he who is in the audience (see 1 John 4:4).

Are your knees still knocking? Then bend them in prayer. Open your Bible and read the promises God gave for such situations as this. You won't necessarily feel less fear. Faith

5. Charles R. Gruner, *Plain Public Speaking* (New York: Macmillan, 1983), pp. 23–25.

is the substance of things hoped for, the evidence of things unseen *and* unfelt (see Heb. 11:1).

I once had a fear of speaking second only to my enormous dread of singing. Every time I sang, my music and voice shook noticeably. Even though I had voice training and experience, my fear silenced me for ten years. Then it became obvious the Lord wanted me to sing again. I had to reckon with my fear. On stage I imagined Jesus standing in the back of the room smiling. I was singing just for him, knowing he heard my heart and not the sour notes. I did not feel less fear, but surrendered and sang off key in front of one hundred women. As I continued to accept singing requests my anxiety decreased, my confidence soared, and my heart sang on key. Emerson knew the truth I discovered: "Do the thing you fear, and death of fear is certain."

Many are the methods to counteract the twitters and jitters of public speaking. Let's take a look at ten of them.

1. *Start small*

Fear is cured by doing the thing you fear. This, however, does not mean filling Carnegie Hall for your testimonial debut. One process with stage fright works like desensitization, in which psychologists introduce the feared object into a room at a comfortable distance from the subject for short periods. The time is gradually increased as the object is brought closer. Likewise, short, successful exposures to speaking in gradually lengthened times reduce fear.

One woman's fear was so great she had never completed even a thirty-second announcement without passing out. Finally, she took a college speech class and warned the instructor about her problem. When she spoke for the first time to introduce herself, she began to sway after about fifteen words. The sensitive instructor encouraged her to take a deep breath and not give up. She continued. By the end of the semester she was able to complete a six-minute speech without fainting.

Start small by raising your hand in Sunday school, making an announcement during a church service, or being a worship leader. This will provide an opportunity to stand in front of a group that is friendly and forgiving, assuring your success. Through this experience you might also become acquainted with a podium and microphone.

Another good experience is having an audience of one. Talking to one person causes less anxiety than does any other speaking situation. Find that person who always has something positive to say. Give her a private preview of your speech, knowing she will be able to point out the good in it. Do not ask someone who will dwell mercilessly on your flaws.

Next, ask for time in Sunday school or in a Bible study group to make a presentation. This will afford the opportunity to become familiar with a written speech under comfortable circumstances. The class will also benefit if you have the right topic.

2. Choose the right topic

Beginning speakers should not tread on unfamiliar ground. The material you pick should fit like a pair of old slippers, comfortable and well-worn; topics with which you are unacquainted only add to prespeech jitters. Additionally, information confidence will improve your delivery. Choosing a topic is discussed in greater depth in the following chapter.

3. Getting off to a good start

The beginning of your speech sets the tone for the entire presentation. There are methods that will break tension and camouflage nervous starts. Humor is one.

Audiences listen better when they anticipate humor. It

grabs their attention and keeps it. This shared laugh immediately establishes a warm rapport and relieves your fear. Many professional speakers use this method to open a speech. Humor, however, does not mean a string of jokes. Usually relating an anecdote or situation will tickle the funny bone and lead naturally into your speech. Many such incidents can be drawn from daily life.

Not everyone feels comfortable nor is successful with the use of humor. If you are not, storytelling is another way to have a smooth beginning. Think about the many things that happen to you. Is there one incident that demonstrates the point of your talk? If you have such a story, it will lend itself to a sincere delivery. A personal experience is easy to relate and has natural emotion and enthusiasm.

Reading a short selection to the audience is another easy way to start your speech. This could be one of many forms: a prayer, Scripture, quotation, poem, an article, or anecdote. The opinion of someone else, especially an authority, adds to your credibility. Reading simplifies your introduction and gives your voice a chance to warm up before attending to other delivery skills.

Whether humor, a story, or a quotation, beginning nerves will be quickly soothed by these introductory methods. Use one of them for a successful start to your next speech.

4. Be *prepared*

Being prepared for a speech is crucial to its success and to your confidence as a speaker. Do you know what you are talking about? You should. Preparedness for a speaker means research and rehearsal.

Research is not as awesome as it sounds. It is simply the gathering of information about your topic. Three areas to examine when looking for information are yourself, the Bible, and other books and people. Studying your topic thoroughly

will greatly increase self-confidence. How to do this is detailed in chapter 3.

On certain days I can be seen standing in front of the
mirror talking enthusiastically into my electric curling iron.
Rehearsing is another important aspect of speech preparation. Speaking into a curling iron is just like talking into
a hand-held mike, something that is awkward the first time.
The mirror, of course, reveals how you look to others. First
practice without the mirror to "feel" the delivery, then watch.
Evaluate your visual performance by using the guidelines
in chapter 9.

Another helpful tool for practicing is the tape recorder.
Record your speech, then listen to it critically. Is yours an
appealing voice? Can you be understood? Evaluate the
quality of your vocal delivery by using the chapter 9
guidelines.

I have a friend who went into holy shock because I practiced my testimony. To her this made me insincere. But
rehearsed does not mean phony. At a luncheon I attended,
Ted Engstrom, president of World Vision International, said
that mediocrity repels rather than draws people to God. He
continued, "Striving for excellence . . . is not only a Christian
duty, but a Christian responsibility."[6]

I agree. As Christians we should give our best for Christ.
In terms of speech giving this means we rehearse. I seriously
doubt any worthwhile minister awakes Sunday morning and
prays, "Okay, Lord, what should I preach about today?" Sermons are prepared often months in advance, themes
planned, and words well-chosen. If you are waiting for inspired words and outstanding talent to drop from heaven
when you reach the podium, you may be disappointed. Some

6. Ted W. Engstrom, "The Pursuit of Excellence" (Address delivered at North-
western College, Roseville, Minnesota, 10 August 1984).

are gifted and some are called. They along with the rest of us need to work hard and be well-prepared.

5. Visual Aids

Sometimes, but not always, using visual aids helps ease initial tensions. Showing the audience a poster, display, or object related to your speech will take the focus off you. Having something at which to point will relax your delivery. Handling a visual aid, however, may make you more nervous. If it does, don't use it. Do what best suits you.

6. Physical condition

As mentioned earlier, fear makes itself known physically, so good physical condition is mandatory for a good delivery. As Mom always said, get lots of sleep, plenty of exercise, and watch what you eat.

Sleep is important, because we need sharp mental faculties when giving a speech. When our autonomic nervous system is preparing us for danger, apparently thinking is not a priority function. When fear strikes, the mind goes blank. I've talked with beginning speakers who, robbed of their presence of mind, had no idea what they said during their speeches. In the case of such a shutdown a tired speaker will have difficulty keeping the mental gears grinding. Sleep will counter this attempt by the consciousness to vacate the premises.

Excess energy is another condition of speech anxiety, and can be countered with physical activity. Once, a student about to give a speech screamed and jumped off the stage. He ran through the auditorium, out the back door, down the hall, reentered backstage, crossed to the podium and announced, "I was just using up my excess energy." I have some better suggestions.

We become geared for enormous physical outlay in our

anticipation of fleeing a stampeding herd of mastodons, but then we just stand there. To avoid this buildup, use as much energy as possible before giving your speech, but not as my student did. Park some distance away from the building and use energy by briskly walking to your destination. Make an extra trip to the powder room. Walk in the hall and get acquainted with members of the audience. This will make the audience seem less like strangers and more like a group of friends.

If during your speech your extra energy is still a problem, take your microphone and walk. Moving will burn up energy as will gesturing with your free hand. Coming from behind the podium creates a closer relationship with the audience, enhances your delivery, aids the mental process, and counters the desire to hide.

Breathlessness is also a result of excess energy. Resist the temptation to sigh. Rather, before speaking take deep diaphragmatic breaths, taking longer to exhale than to inhale. This will soothe the nervous system.

Another manifestation of excess energy is talking too fast. It is almost impossible to talk faster than we can comprehend; however, you must still be heard and understood. The faster you talk, the more perfect your articulation must be; use of pauses must increase and so should volume. Listeners are lazy. Don't make them work hard by your talking too fast.

Eating and drinking may be hazardous to your speech. Unfortunately, many speaking engagements follow banquets and luncheons. Erma Bombeck suggests, "Feed a cold crowd, starve a speaker."[7] She is right. The flight-or-fight mechanism stops digestion, much the same way our bodies gear down digestion before delivering a baby. So don't ov-

---

7. Bombeck, "A practiced speaker."

erload your stomach; it may rebel. Avoid tea, coffee, cola,
and other caffeinated products; they cause shaking. Remembering my professional-speaker friend, avoid water, too! The
best thing to do for a thirst is to have a lemon drop before
speaking.

7. Mind control

Anything can happen when fear gets a foothold in your
mind. Something or someone will control your mind; it
should be you. One incident poignantly illustrates this. Two
American soldiers were captured during the Korean War.
Both were taken into an interrogation room. One was blindfolded and tied to a table. The other was seated and made
to watch. The wrists of the blindfolded soldier were slit with
a knife, and he bled to death in seven minutes. Then the
soldier watching was blindfolded and tied to the same table.
Instead of a knife a piece of sharp ice was drawn across his
wrists, and warm water dripped from the "cut." He died in
ten minutes and never shed a drop of blood. He believed
himself into death.

Public speaking is not a life-and-death issue, but sometimes we act as though it is. The soldier's experience demonstrates the power our minds have. If we surrender to fear,
that power will be used against us. But if we give our minds
to God, he will use them for his work. "Thou wilt keep *him*
in perfect peace, *whose* mind *is* stayed *on thee . . .*" (Isa. 26:3,
KJV, ital. added).

On what is your mind stayed? Are you imagining all the
things that could go wrong? Are you concerned about trip-
ping on the stage, choking on your water, or someone crit-
icizing you? You can play the "what if" game and worry
yourself speechless. Worry is just another form of fear; it is
believing yourself into failure.

Dr. Robert Du Pont, president of the Phobia Society of

America, suggests replacing the "what ifs" with "so what!" Yes, *so what* if something goes wrong? You will live through it. We may not *be* the best, but if we *do* our best, that's what counts with God. The rest will come.

Instead of thinking "what if," we need to behave "as if." This principle was developed by William James who introduced psychology to this country. His theory states that to feel brave you must act brave, and courage will replace fear.[8] Yet, too many Christians mistakenly believe that to act contrary to the way you feel is to be dishonest. I have heard numerous novice speakers begin a speech with, "I don't believe how nervous I am!" This alarms and disappoints the audience. As a speaker it is better to display phony confidence than genuine fear. The audience really doesn't want to know you are nervous. If you approach the podium and face the audience confidently, eventually how you act will replace how you feel.

Has someone said you'll never make it as a speaker, and you believed it? Instead, believe that with God you can do anything. Faith will open the floodgates of your potential. I like what motivational speaker and former Congressman Ed Foreman has to say:

> According to recognized aeronautical tests, the Bumble Bee cannot fly because of the shape and weight of his body in relation to his total wing area. The Bumble Bee doesn't know this; so he goes ahead and flies anyway.[9]

Go ahead and fly! Do the impossible: be a speaker. "With men this is impossible, but with God all things are possible" (Matt. 19:26).

8. Norman Vincent Peale, "Stop Feeling Tired — Start Having Energy," *Creative Help for Daily Living* (October 1982):20.

9. Ed Foreman, *The Daily Menu for Laughing, Loving, and Living* (Dallas).

8. Be *audience-centered, not self-centered*

A speaker was dressed in her best clothes prior to leaving for a speaking engagement. She was anxious and quickly trying to prepare her children for the babysitter. Her rushing came to an abrupt halt when the baby spit up on her. Looking upward she prayed, "Thank you, Lord. I was caught up in myself."

What a marvelous attitude. Often fear is caused by too much focus on self. But it is the audience with whom you should be concerned. You cannot best serve your audience by worrying about the run in your pantyhose. No one else cares.

A letter from a former speech student expresses the depth from which a speaker can rise.

> As a child I was always the one who wouldn't raise her hand in school to answer a question, because of all the attention it would focus on me. I couldn't stand being in the limelight. I always felt that I dressed too poorly, looked too unattractive, etc., to be favorably received by anyone. Teachers were sometimes short tempered and ridiculed kids if they gave the wrong answer. It was just easier all the way around not to try to answer, and to try to hide so that they wouldn't call on me. From childhood on I always tried to avoid *any* situation that called for a solo in public.[10]

She went on to be a frequent speaker and founder of a worldwide organization.

Pulitzer Prize winning author Annie Dillard says, "Self-consciousness . . . is the one instrument that unplugs all the rest.[11] The self-conscious speaker is disconnected from the

10. Pat Brewer (Letter).
11. Annie Dillard, *Pilgrim at Tinker Creek* (New York: Harper Magazine Press, 1974), p. 82.

audience and unplugged from God. If the speaker's focus is, "How can I draw the audience to God?" rather than "What are they thinking of me?" self-consciousness will not be a problem.

9. Visit the scene

Before the day of the meeting, go to the place where you will be speaking. Walk on the stage, look into the empty seats, handle the microphone, and familiarize yourself with the podium and backstage area. If you are speaking at some distance from home, arrive early. Explore the speaking area in advance, then leave until your scheduled arrival time. When you are announced and walk across the platform, you will feel at home and there will be no last-minute surprises.

10. Be yourself

When asked, "What is happiness?" an elementary-school boy responded, "Being myself." We all feel the need to be okay just as we are, accepted rather than criticized. As Bill Cosby says, "No one fits in a pigeonhole except a pigeon."[12] It takes a lot of energy to maintain a facade, and trying to be someone else only adds pressure to a speaking situation.

Once, I wanted to sound like an extra-sweet, creampuff Christian, so I practiced speaking slowly in a soft, melodic voice. This was difficult, since I tend to be naturally bois-terous. I recorded and played back this newly found voice. It sounded just like what it was — phony.

There is a big difference between being an imitation of someone else and being the best, professional you. Ges-turing like an evangelist, voicing words like an anchor-woman, and dressing like a model are not going to make you a grand speaker. You are an individual, and as such you

12. Bill Cosby, *Decker Communications Report* (February 1985):7.

are valuable to God. Don't polish away the reflection of your uniqueness by being a poor copy of someone else.

I have briefly touched many topics that the following chapters cover in detail. Experiment and study further to find the method that makes you most comfortable when addressing an audience. Don't let the flutters get you down. Whip those butterflies into formation. "Fear not," said the Lord. "I am with you always . . ." (Matt. 28:20), even until the end of your speech.

Work Sheet

1. Examine your greatest public-speaking fears. Reexamine your self-images. Which self-image is threatened? What can you do to secure that self-image? Put your answer into practice.
2. Imagine the most humiliating thing that could happen to you during a speech. Think your way through the details and emotions. Visualize the audience's response and your feelings and actions in the situation. Can you do anything to prevent this from happening? If you can't, how can you modify your response to what *might* take place? Imagine your response if this same circumstance happened to another speaker.
3. Read the following selections from Scripture and commit them to memory for use in times of fear: 2 Timothy 1:7, Deuteronomy 1:17, Psalm 27:1, Psalm 118:6, Joshua 1:9, Matthew 8:26, Matthew 10:31, and Romans 8:37.
4. As children of God, we have power over the spirit of fear. Bind that spirit by praying out loud when anxiety overtakes you.

3

Do I Have Anything to Say?
Discovering and researching your topic

We speak that which we know, and bear witness of that which we have seen.

John 3:11

At this point you are probably thinking, "Maybe, I just might, possibly, somehow, someday, overcome my fear enough to talk." But now fear dons a new form and a gargantuan roadblock looms on the highway ahead: "Do I have anything to say?"

When I was asked to make my first speech, my reaction was typical: panic. I felt like a minus fifteen on a holiness scale of one to ten. I wondered what I, a Johnny-come-lately, could say to an audience of women who had been Christians since before I was born. All I had were training wings, and I surely wasn't ready to mount up on wings of an eagle.

Most baby birds fly because they are kicked out of the nest. Most speakers learn to speak because they are pushed to the podium.

I had spent twenty-eight years in the secular trenches, and as a seven-year-old Christian felt my inadequacies. I had to keep reminding myself that God is glorified in our weakness (2 Cor. 12:9). Fortunately, a Christian's credibility does not depend on academic degrees or success, but on a life lived with Christ, no matter when that new life was birthed.

Every Christian life is a message from God. "The great sin," says Nobel laureate Mother Teresa, "is the sin of disbelief in the potential powers of the human soul."[1] We feel uninteresting, unworthy, and inadequate. Others overcome enormous handicaps, experience miracles, or dramatic conversions, but we think our lives dull by comparison. This overdone modesty is the greatest stumbling block to would-be Christian speakers.

"Oh, but who would want to hear about me?" the doubter asks. You must think someone does, or you wouldn't be reading this book! Maybe someone has already invited you to speak. She must think you have something to offer. No one has called? Maybe God is calling.

Don't underestimate yourself as God's vessel. Second guessing only depletes energy and creative reserves. If you have hope to offer, you have something to say; if you have faith to offer, you have something to say; and if you have love to give, you are singing God's song. Now, what do you have to say? Plenty!

Whether of triumph, tragedy, or tedium, everyone (that includes you) has a story to tell. Maybe you started college

1. Curtis Bill Pepper, "I'm a Little Pencil in God's Hand," *McCall's* (March 1980):82.

at forty and struggled with pride or the daily tasks of being a housewife. Others are privately struggling in the same way. They need to know you traveled the road before them. What you have lived, whether great or small by your standards, is your area of expertise. "Your life is your message."[2]

In this chapter you will begin to discover and develop a core speech. This is a compilation of what you have lived and observed, of your interactions with others and with God. From this core many types of speeches will grow and be modified for a variety of speaking situations.

Perspective

From your horn of plenty a topic or theme must be selected. This choice is the first mental step in speech writing. The topic or theme (I use these terms interchangably) does not need to be new. It doesn't matter whether all the magazines have written about it or Phil Donahue has talked about it; your firsthand experience brings a new perspective no one else can offer. No one has seen life through your eyes but you.

To demonstrate the individuality of perspective, examine figure 1. Gaze at it for a minute. What do you see?

The responses to this figure that I have heard vary greatly. Some see two men, others a man and a woman, a wad of paper, an egg timer, an end table. One young man saw a nuclear cloud. If the concrete is seen in so many different ways, think how much more varied are the views of life's intangibles — spiritual issues, relationships, and emotions. As a speaker, you have a topic that is unique in its perspective. Where someone sees a nuclear cloud, you may see a silver lining.

2. Quin Sherrer, "Who Is Jamie Buckingham?" *The Christian Writer* (August 1984):15.

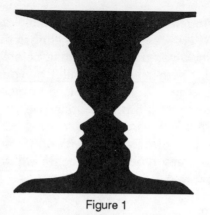

Figure 1

The thread

All speeches must have a single theme or common thread around which a beginning, middle, and end are structured. (All the material included in the speech must relate to or support this theme.) In every life there is often a chronology of events or a common theme that recurs. The search for a speech theme begins with you. Let me demonstrate.

One day my husband brought home a piece of telephone cable. On the outside it was black and ordinary looking, nothing particularly exciting. Turning the cable, I viewed the exposed end. Then I saw stubs of more than one hundred tiny, color-coated wires running through it. At first it looked like a mass of colors swirled together carelessly. Upon closer examination lovely hues of red, orange, blue, and purple came into view. Each wire ran the full length of the section of casing. If grasped by my fingertips a single delicate wire could be removed from the mass and its individual color exposed.

Our lives are that way. On the outside we look ordinary enough, nothing particularly exciting. But look inside the casing, expose your private sanctuary, the place where life has left its many colored threads. At first you may see only a complexity of interwoven spiritual, emotional, and social threads. But look more closely. There are greens, reds, and blacks that run the length of your life. Reach in and pull one out.

Introspection is the process by which I began to search for my thread. I found, as you may, that there were several, but one was colored more brightly than the rest. It beckoned to be pulled and exposed. In my self-exploration I discovered burial grounds of events and emotions. Throwing out my rose-colored glasses, I relived my past, seeing the lacks and losses, the loves and blessings, the breakings and mendings.

Following this process I said to my husband, "I can't believe I survived all this!" There was my thread: losses survived. This was what I knew, what I had lived, where my credibility lay. I titled my testimony "Gaining Through Losing," borrowed from the excellent book by Evelyn Christenson.[3] I had hope to offer those who suffered.

This is the way you should start. Examine your life from beginning to end. What is your common thread?

Brainstorming

To answer the above question, get a pencil and paper. Read the following list of brainstorming questions and respond spontaneously. Don't dwell on any particular question for too long. Just write down in a single word or phrase the first thought it triggers; then move on to the next question. Spend five minutes writing all the ideas that come to mind. Do not be concerned with whether these are good speech topics; only try to get at the least a dozen thoughts, or as many as fifty. Write whatever comes to mind and wrap the

3. Evelyn Christenson, *Gaining Through Losing* (Wheaton, Ill.: Victor Books, 1981).

process in prayer. Ask God to reveal to you what he would have you talk about, and he will. "Commit your works to the LORD, and your plans will be established" (Prov. 16:3).

Some of you may already know what God wants you to tell. There was a life-changing event, a dramatic conversion, or some other obvious move by God. Do the exercise anyway, and you will find more ideas. Buried in your life is the hand of God gone unrecognized.

Brainstorming List

1. How do I spend the major portion of my time?
2. Am I blessed with good health, or plagued by illness?
3. Do I have a special concern for the elderly, handicapped, children?
4. Have I creative talents or organizational skills?
5. Is there a thorn in my side?
6. Has my life revolved around athletic skills, or clumsiness?
7. Has my life been one of service, or being served?
8. Have I experienced multiple losses, or inordinate success?
9. Do I have a special way with pets, plants, or people?
10. Did one major event or person color my entire life?
11. Do I wear a special label such as handicapped, pastor's wife, or homely?
12. Are grief, joy, or pain my companions?
13. What work have I done: salaried, volunteer, church, or home?
14. Has there been a special ministry in my life or someone special who ministered to me?
15. Have I struggled financially, or been richly blessed?
16. Has my life been ordinary, or extraordinary?

You now have identified some dominant threads. There could be many colors to your life. Maybe you find your life filled with stray cats (#3) and lost human beings (#9), and in spite of a physical handicap (#11) have successfully served (#7) many. Possibly your life is a series of dramatic events (#16), or your life has been a happy one (#12) because of the legacy of a loving parent (#10). These thoughts translate into themes.

If you found yourself struggling with this exercise, there are other idea sources. Sometimes we are so involved with living we are blind to the valuable example we are setting in little, everyday ways. Ask a friend or relative what they see happening in your life. You will be surprised. What you have to offer is often more obvious to others than to yourself.

Another person you might ask for speech suggestions is the person who invited you to speak, or who recommended you. They must see something in your life that is worth telling. For instance, I recommended a friend as a speaker. She had gone through seeing the slow death of her young son to cancer, yet she emerged glowing. When most people would be bitter and hateful, her voice rang with peace and joy — a remarkable woman sustained by a remarkable God.

Sort through your brainstorming answers and suggestions. Narrow your topic choices to the five most dominant. Maybe there are no lifelong themes. Possibly you can see a cause-and-effect such as a ministry to neighbor children because you were laid off work. From your five choices pick the theme that appeals to you most. Next, read the following six questions. If your theme cannot elicit an answer of yes to each, then try other themes until one passes the six-point test. But save all your ideas for future use. They are the groundwork upon which other speeches will be built.

Six-point Test

1. Does this information have universal appeal?

Universal themes such as love, self-esteem, and salvation, are basic to all human life. They cut across racial, cultural, and religious lines. When I asked international speaker Florence Littauer what advice she would give beginning speakers, she stated, "The first question you should ask yourself is, 'What do I have to say?' (You have just done that in the brainstorming exercise.) The second question should be, 'Does anyone need to hear it?' "[4]

Do they? Does your information relate to others? Your topic should relate to the audience, not just to you. Can this speech be developed to meet the needs or interests of most Christians without excluding or alienating the undecided?

2. Do I have victory in this area of my life?

Talking about areas of unresolved conflict in your life is unwise. Resolved does not mean perfected; but the path must be clearly marked, spiritually controlled, and on the upswing.

There are several reasons to avoid such topics. If you are still involved in a problem, chances are that negative emotional overtones will cast a shadow on your talk. Once, I wrote a book proposal and gave it to an editor. After reading two chapters she handed it back in distaste, much like holding a dead mouse by its tail. I realized without being told; my tale was just as bad. It was the sarcastic outpouring of anger, frustration, and self-pity. In retrospect, I'm relieved no one else read it! I was still too emotionally involved in the issue to present it inoffensively.

4. Florence Littauer (Letter to the author).

Speakers have the same heat-of-the-moment reactions. Beginners often amaze themselves with tears that flow uncontrollably during a speech. When we start tilling the soil of the past, the pungent odor of decomposing pain burns in our throats. Our gardens that bloom so colorfully on the surface are often rooted in the rotten, decomposing matter of our lives. There is nothing wrong with emotion or tears. Too many negative feelings, however, may indicate victory is not yet in hand.

3. Can I show without preaching?

A topic based on one magazine article with a few Scripture texts thrown in will become a bad sermon. Preaching *at* listeners is negative and condescending by nature. It alienates audiences. Show, don't tell.

To show a message it must be demonstrated through life, not through abstractions — and preferably your life. Can you see the theme in the events of your life? Albert Schweitzer said, "Example is not the main thing in influencing others. It is the only thing."[5] What you live you know best. Have you learned to live with pain, overcome boredom, or be an intercessor? Your experience will infuse your presentation with a vitality that book study will never give. No matter how mundane your life may seem, someone else is living there, too.

If you are not directly involved in living your topic, can you demonstrate your point through the experiences of friends, students, or family? Perhaps your topic is the need for prison ministries. You were never arrested for criminal action, but your church has a prison ministry in which you are involved. You can draw upon your observations of the pain of imprisonment, the spiritual needs of inmates and

5. Erica Anderson, *The World of Albert Schweitzer* (New York, 1955), p. 138.

how they were met. The more you can show through first-hand observation, the better.

4. Will this speech insult or injure others?

One reason not to discuss some areas of your life is the people involved. They would not want you to mention them or your negative opinions of their actions. We must preserve the dignity of individuals, organizations, and other Christian denominations, or lose the respect of all. Steer clear of doctrinal and controversial issues, unless giving a speech to persuade (see Chapter 8). Sometimes an issue does need to be confronted, but only when the situation is appropriate and the motivation pure. Generally there is nothing more damaging to the faith than Christians being critical of other Christians.

Are you pointing a blaming finger? Are you seeing their splinter and not your log? Is a judgmental tone creeping into your voice? Shrink from criticism, even if you think the rotten bums deserve it! Remember, you are sometimes wrong, too.

5. Will anyone be helped?

The public platform is not the place to gather sympathy by unloading our problems. Our job is to serve; even secularists know this. Bert Decker in his monthly "Decker Communications Report" says, "Forget about job titles — we're all in service to others. . . . The better your speaking serves others' needs, the better job you're doing — and the more results you'll get." He continues, "There are two key questions to ask yourself before any presentation or interview: (1) What do my listeners *need* to know? and (2) What will help them the most? As Albert Einstein said, 'The purpose of man is to serve man.' "[6]

6. Bert Decker, "Speaking Should Serve Others," *Decker Communications Report* (February 1985):2.

As Christians our job is to offer hope and skills for living and coping; and to the non-Christian who will be in every audience we need to offer the lifesaving good news. Does your story do that?

6. *Where is God?*

Many people ask this question, especially in times of trouble. Big bucks and big names are made claiming God is there; the people making them, however, leave the impression he is impotent in controlling the world he created. But anyone who has read the Bible with any attention knows God is our help, our strength in time of trouble, and he *is* omnipotently in control. When speaking we need to show his controlling hand through our lives. Can God be seen at work in what you relate?

People are interested in people, but your experiences should point to God's power through your life, not to you. Can you imagine him applauding everything you say? Would he smile at your humor and approve of your description of that person who hurt you?

Your boldness should reflect God's glory — his love in your pain, his joy in your ordinariness, his support in your human failing. Don't just tell us he is there; show us when and how he is there for everyone. If you close your talk with a spirited rendition of the song "I Did It My Way," you have failed.

Missing a few of the above six questions does not mean a theme must automatically be tossed out. A theme that passes four or five points still has potential, but you immediately see where its weaknesses are.

If you do not have a theme that will develop into a short talk, or if you feel the topic is not right for you, then look at your brainstorming sheet and try another idea, several if necessary, before making a final decision. (For purposes of doing the additional exercises in this chapter, be sure to make a choice. After your speech is written, the six-point test can again act as a final check.)

Reliving on Paper

Now that you have decided on an idea, it is time to make a list of everything from your experience that relates to your theme. Is your theme patience? List all the frustrations that helped you grow. One woman related that she prayed for patience and God gave her twins. Is it coping with a handicapped child? List the memorable moments — sweet and sour, doubts, despairs, triumphs, and defeats. Have you always had a soft spot for the elderly? How did it start? Write your first recollections of this feeling and consequent contacts and outreach. Journey back in time and unlock the memory box that hides your theme.

No Christian is threadbare. There is a finely woven pattern that moved you from then to now. Pray and think; there is much in your years that can be used in developing your talk. Ask yourself: When was I right and when was I wrong? What resulted? When did God leave his footprints in my circumstances? When did he send friends to minister? When did he send someone in need to me? List anecdotes, thoughts, observations, experiences, sermons, anyone, anything that might relate.

Just because you are recording all this material does not mean you must use it. Your garden will be weeded and organized in the next chapter.

Filling your cup

Once you have related and reacted to your life and theme and poured yourself onto paper, it is time to examine your theme with different eyes. Are your ideas on this topic consistent with God's? Are you waltzing with thoughts contrary to Scripture? Do you teach as doctrine the precepts of man (see Isa. 29:13; Matt. 15:9)?

When asking yourself these questions go directly to the Bible. Do not pass through other books, and do not collect their ideas. Too often we lack spiritual confidence and think we cannot understand Scripture without someone else's interpretation tacked to it. It is profitable to be actively involved in a Bible study with others, but we also must be confident the Holy Spirit is our teacher (see John 14:26). A pure-hearted search of the Bible will reveal God's message to each of us. Ideas of others (this will come later) cloud our minds, making it more difficult to hear from God. So, initially go to the basic source.[7]

In *Lord, Change Me!* Evelyn Christenson explains the process by which she hears from God:

> Staying in the Scripture for instruction, I would read only until He spoke. Then I would stop to pray about what He had said, analyze His reason for stopping me at that particular point, discover the need He knew I had, and then determine what I could do to change.[8]

Another way to hear God's message without an interpreter is to check a concordance. It is similar to a dictionary, listing the words of the Bible. By looking up a word such as suffering, all the Scripture texts containing this term will be at your disposal. There are numerous types of concordances on the market, from the bulky, inclusive Strong's to paperbacks. Some Bibles also contain partial concordances. These are handy and help locate information quickly. Check your

---

7. Willard A. Scofield, "Scriptures in Writing" (Workshop held at the Decision School of Christian Writing, 8 August 1984).

8. Evelyn Christenson, "*Lord, Change Me!*" (Wheaton, Ill.: Victor Books, 1977), p. 23.

local Bible bookstore for a companion concordance for your particular version of the Bible.

Once God's Word on your topic is firmly rooted in your mind, it is time to go to other sources: books, authorities, and friends.

Bible handbooks, dictionaries, commentaries, and study guides abound. Each offers clearer understanding of Scripture and is a helpful resource. If after study you do not understand a passage, you may then want to refer to one of these books for clarification. But Bible scholars are not the only sources of understanding God. Other people, authors, or friends are just as useful. Often their lives are exemplary, whether they have written about them or not.

When I was researching the topic of my first speech, I found that noted authors such as Philip Yancy, Evelyn Christenson, and Joyce Landorf had also wrestled with losses, but the life of my friend who lost a son gave me more insight into the positive aspects of grief than all the authorities put together. It is often the persons whose spirits are in tune with God's who can be the greatest resources when you are putting together God's message through your life. You will know them by their fruit. But if they claim to be pear trees and produce lemons, look out!

Your research need not be costly. Instead of purchasing all the printed materials, check with your minister; he or the church library may have books you need. Public libraries usually carry religious magazines. There are also indexes that list magazine articles by topic. Ask your librarian.

Friends may also have books or magazines that examine your topic. My friends often loan me books because they know I'm interested in a particular subject. Quite often it is just what the Lord wants me to read.

Be alert to newspaper stories, broadcasts, and lives that cross your path demonstrating the principles you are researching. Record Scripture passages and other information that relate to your theme. As you collect them be sure to document your sources.

Now you may be wondering, if this is *my* story, *my* testimony, why do I have to do all this reading and studying? Knowledge is equipment. Speech building requires tools. Just as you cannot dig a basement with a teaspoon, so you cannot build a speech without wisdom. One professional speaker told me she has ten hours of information for a one-hour talk!

I always like to consider a topic from all perspectives before I try to show it to someone else. Researching helped me see grief through the eyes of others. It was a thought-provoking check point, guarding against my misrepresenting God because of my own ignorance. Other person's lives show alternate viewpoints that may strengthen or weaken ours. It is important to know others will disagree with our ideas and why. Most important, we want to be consistent with Scripture.

Your cup is now full. You know yourself and your topic and are ready to write. But first, there is one final point to consider.

The final exam

One summer I attended a writers' workshop offered by Lois Johnson, author of several books including *Falling Apart or Coming Together*.[9] At the time, she was in the process of writing that book. She warned the students (most of whom were fledgling writers), "When you decide to write about a topic, look out for the testings." She went on to explain that she went through much falling apart before her book came together. I found this hard to believe.

9. Lois Johnson, *Falling Apart or Coming Together: How You Can Experience the Faithfulness of God* (Minneapolis: Augsburg, 1984).

When I chose my speech topic mentioned earlier, "Gaining Through Losing," it was because I had already passed the testing, or so I thought. That year I had watched my mother die from cancer, suffered my own poor health and other personal losses. I thought I had passed through the valley. But between the time I chose my topic in October and gave my speech in January, I was to know even more loss.

On Thanksgiving Day we were sloshing through five hundred gallons of water and ashes left from our house fire a few days before. As we tried to restore our home and move back in before Christmas my heart ached. It was truly a devastating year in my life. Yet, knowing I *had* to offer hope to other women in January forced me to not give up my search for a silver lining in my nuclear cloud. It was the commitment to speak that caused me to not cave in emotionally. I survived another loss victoriously.

Coincidence? Testing? You decide.

Work Sheet

1. Begin keeping a journal of emotions, events, and spiritual growth. After several months of writing what is on your mind, you will begin to see God's answers and dealings. This will give you future threads from which to draw speech topics. Two resources are *Write to Discover Yourself*, by Ruth Vaughn[10] and *How to Keep a Spiritual Journal*, by Ronald Klug.[11]

2. Examine areas of your life where you do not have victory. Pray, and be alert to possible solutions in scripture. Quite often our struggles can hold the answers

---

10. Ruth Vaughn, *Write to Discover Yourself* (Garden City, N.Y.: Doubleday, 1980).
11. Ronald Klug, *How to Keep a Spiritual Journal* (Nashville: Nelson, 1982).

to someone else's problems and could be used in future speeches.

3. After doing the activities in this chapter, set aside your ideas for one or two weeks to allow them to "cool." Reexamine them at this later time and you will be able to see even more ideas and possibilities.

Part **2**

Plan

4

Getting It All Together
Organizing your speech

Many are the plans in a man's heart, but it is the LORD's purpose that prevails.

Proverbs 19:21, NIV

Now that you have a topic it is time to embark on a $100,000 career — speech writing. Writing your story may be the extent of your career or just the beginning. Many, like Joseph J. Kelley, Jr., make it their life's work. It is a valuable skill in the public arena. This professional, who has written for Presidents, has this to say about speech writing:

Some of the clearest and best is from people who were never touched by the ivy on collegiate halls.[1]

1. Joseph J. Kelley, *Speechwriting: The Master Touch* (Harrisburg, Pa.: Stackpole, 1980), p. 10.

So do not be intimidated if you are not a college graduate. Throw out your bag of excuses. You may not be writing the state of the union address, but you are writing the state of the soul address, which is eternally more important.

The Plan

God had a plan and a schedule when he put the universe in place. In speech writing we can do no less. "The mind of man plans his way, but the LORD directs his steps" (Prov. 16:9). Our responsibility is to plan. God will take care of the results.

If you know how to type, you know the experience of your finger hitting the wrong key before you can stop it. The mouth makes the same mistakes. It will betray you with wrong, spur-of-the-moment comments before you can react. Following a well-prepared outline will counter this impulse to express whatever pops into your head. When writing there is still time for corrections; when speaking there is no second chance. Once those words escape your mouth, there is no atmospheric eraser, just a big verbal typo.

Any prespeech organization is better than a top-of-the-head impromptu. If you miss the mark, God *may* drop a few right words into your mouth. Then again, he may not intercede, but allow your mistakes to nourish your growth. Ouch! Robert Schuller would call that an ego blowout in public.

The following are steps for developing *any* type of speech:

1. Choose and narrow your topic.
2. Decide on a goal.
3. Choose main points.
4. Organize the points.
5. Develop speech-body specifics.
6. Write a conclusion.
7. Write an introduction.

Steps 1 through 6 will be covered in the remainder of this chapter. Step 7 is in the following chapter because it deserves special attention. The introduction serves the important functions of gaining the audience's attention and changing to adapt to each audience, situation, and occasion. The rest of the speech requires only minor changes to adapt to these variables.

1. Narrowing the topic

In chapter 3 you gathered raw material from your life and other sources. Now you have floods of information on your topic. With that done, the rest is as easy as baking cookies. You have decided on chocolate chip and pull that card from your recipe box. Following a speech recipe is no different. You need to know what ingredients to include, the order in which to mix for best results, and how long to bake. All are important. And just like burned cookies, an overdone audience will shrivel and harden, too!

Consider your accumulated experiences and research as ingredients. Among them may be onions, oregano, and orange slices. But just because they are spicy and found in the kitchen does not mean these ingredients can be mixed together and produce cookies.

For example, when I was asked to speak at a mother and daughter banquet, I had a hard time whittling down my material to thirty minutes. I wanted to tell about my birthday back in 1981 when I was sitting by the lake praying as I watched the herring gulls circling overhead. I wanted to tell how a Scripture verse about wings came to mind, how I rushed home and tried to find it but couldn't; how that night I went to the movie *Chariots of Fire* and Isaiah 40:31: "mounting up on eagle wings" was read. It was so exciting to me, but unnecessary for the audience's understanding of my point. It also eliminated ten minutes when I cut it out of my speech.

Experienced speakers are sometimes guilty of trying to add spice to a speech with information that has no business being there. They go off on tangents or stroll down memory lane, leaving the audience behind. I remember one professional who was supposed to tell how to write for newspapers. After his making leading remarks about newspapers, he spent the next hour talking about something else.

To eliminate unnecessary information from your speech, your topic must be narrowed and focussed. Everything about love, for instance, cannot be covered in one talk. Love may be the strong factor in your life, the thread that is constant, but the focus of such a topic must be limited.

Every topic has multiple points, but they cannot all be included in one speech. To narrow a topic, you must first identify these points. Using the topic *love*, let's study the process by which it can be divided into its multiple points.

Diagram 1 shows the many aspects of the topic *love*. There

Diagram 1

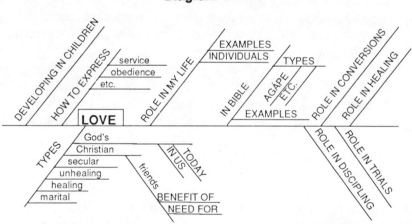

are numerous divisions and subdivisions. You may see even more possibilities. Obviously, from the vast amount of information, a speech on everything about love could go on for days. But by your choosing one aspect the topic is narrowed and so is the speaking time necessary to cover it. The following are some possible speech topics taken from diagram 1:

1. Love of Christian friends is strength in time of trials.
2. How God used my child to minister love to many.
3. Loving relationships: the key to mental health.
4. Christian love changes lives.
5. The role of agápe love in conversion and discipling.

Now it is time to diagram your speech. On a piece of paper, place your single-word topic (or short phrase) in a box. This is the broadest aspect of the topic. Divide and subdivide it, developing as many specific minor points as possible. The diagram progresses from general to specific. Use diagram 2 as a guide.

Now, before choosing the final points of your speech, put

Diagram 2

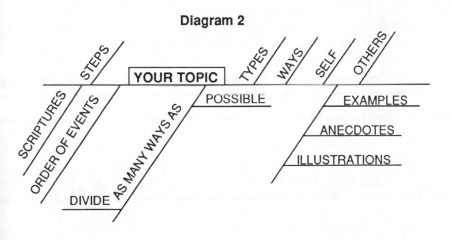

your diagram aside to consider another aspect of speech writing: your goal.

2. Hitting the mark

An arrow cannot hit a bullseye without a target; a runner cannot win a marathon without a finish line; a batter cannot score a run without a home plate. The target, finish line, and home plate are goals. A speaker must have a goal, too.

The speaker's goal falls within the human spirit and is not as easily seen as the athlete's. Your goal is a specific audience response. Would you like the listeners to feel their burdens have been shared, their lives redirected, their appreciation of this country renewed? Is your goal for them to become more involved with their spouses, children, or church? Do you want to change their minds on a particular issue, inform them of a new ministry, or show them how to survive trials? The targeted response will be hit if it is clearly focussed in your mind. How would you have your audience grow?

One woman addressed two thousand businessmen and businesswomen who had paid handsomely to hear her and her husband speak. She began with business, but then wandered off the subject. It soon became obvious she had run out of things to say, especially when she asked the audience what they wanted to hear. A few people shouted out issues that she addressed briefly, followed by twenty minutes about her children. This woman obviously had planned nothing for this speaking engagement, had no goals in mind, and surely didn't hit one. What is even more amazing is that two thousand people would be kind enough to listen to her for an hour and a half!

One of your goals should be the audience's retention of the information you give. If the audience is overloaded, a mental circuit will blow out and the message won't compute. Listeners cannot relisten to a speech the way readers can reread a difficult paragraph. Neither can they stop you while they check the dictionary for an unfamiliar term. Therefore, you need to simplify the message in every way to facilitate listener comprehension.

3. *The backbone*

Two things are common to all speeches, whether they are two-minute announcements, or two-hour presentations. The first is the topic or theme, which we have already discussed. The second is the structure of beginning, middle, and end around which the theme is built.

The topic is the backbone of your speech. Visualize for a moment the human skeletal system. The head would have nothing on which to balance without the vertebrae below. The legs would have no function without their connection to the bony structures adjacent to the vertebral column. Everything connects at the backbone.

Housed within this hollow backbone are the nerves. They extend to all parts of the body, sending and returning messages to and from the fingers and toes. A speech is the same. Individual comments are like nerve endings that must come back and connect their messages with the main theme.

The human backbone is composed of twenty-six vertebrae. The speech backbone is built of only three to five main points. The number of points you choose from your diagram to support the theme should always be limited to five or less. The reason is simple. The average listener cannot attend to, process, and remember more. For example, do you know the twenty-seven books of the New Testament in order? Out of order? The first time you heard them, did you remember them automatically? If so, you are remarkable! How about the Beatitudes, the Ten Comandments? Can you snap those right off? (You may add a few more points in a classroom situation where students are taking notes or where you use a handout or visual aids.)

Examine the diagram of your topic again. What are the strongest points that you want to make? Which ones move your audience closer to your goal? Decide, and take out everything else from this speech and tuck it away for future use.

Now go back and choose your main points before continuing.

4. Body building

There are as many ways to organize the body of a speech as there are speakers. Thinking of the points as vertebrae, you can stack them together any way you like. You may order your points in an outline by chronology, size, or however they seem to logically flow together.

The purpose of an outline is to help you the speaker remember what to say and to aid the writing process. A logically sequenced outline also guides the listener through the speech with ease.

Many speakers enjoy using all the same beginning letters in their outline. This helps both the speaker and the audience remember better. The leader of a workshop on journaling used these four terms as her outline:

1. Memorials (journals are)
2. Models (showed some)
3. Mangos (produce fruit)
4. Mechanics (how to keep a journal)[2]

2. Gail MacDonald, "Reflecting on Your Walk with God" (Workshop held in Wheaton, Ill., 10 July 1985).

One Bible-study teacher used this outline:

1. Conquering through Christ
2. Commendation from God
3. Competence by Holy Spirit[3]

Evelyn Christenson said she usually uses a three-point outline. In her workshop on prayer she did something a little different. Her outline was simply to address four of the questions most often asked about prayer. These called for no special sequence.

When I judged a national speech contest, I found that the speeches which flowed smoothly were well-organized and liberally dosed with transitions. Transitions are the adhesive that glues speech points together. Some are more obvious than others. A list of transitions is included in chapter 6.

5. *The flesh*

To flesh out the bony structure of your speech, choose supporting information that best achieves your desired audience response. The professional speaker is able to do this by focussing on the trees and ignoring the forest. The novice looks at the forest and sees not only the trees, but also the grass, weeds, flowers, fallen leaves, moss, squirrel, chipmunk, and mosquitoes. (Sigh!) She then tries to talk about all of them in one speech. They are all in the forest, but don't put every detail in your speech.

Once the order of your points is decided, specifics can be added. From your notes sift out choice ideas, anecdotes, illustrations, experiences, quotations, and research results that demonstrate or support your main points and build

3. Myrl Glochner (Bible study conducted in Wheaton, Ill., 11 July 1985).

toward your goal. One fellow gave a speech to recruit army volunteers. He marched the audience through his first day in the army step by step — his haircut, physical, innoculations, clothes issued, locker, bunk, first meal in the mess hall, and on and on. None of this gave anyone reason to want to join the military and therefore did not support his main point.

Your life is the best source for the meat of your speech. Look through your notes for those incidents related to your theme. They have eye-witness credibility and are easiest to relate because of your firsthand experience. For example, when teaching the importance of time in delivering a speech, I always tell about the group of teachers who walked out on me when the school bell rang. This shows my personal involvement (and humiliation!) in the point I am illustrating.

It is God in you who really needs to be seen, even though people are interested in people. Choose the most vivid experiences from your life that also show him. But be careful not to outglow his glory. Your God thread must be the most obvious.

Know you are in agreement with the Bible. Show how Scripture supports your ideas. Those who are familiar with Scripture will recognize the truth without the reference; for others the occasional references are necessary validation of your claims.

Next use the experience and knowledge of others. If an author or authority supports your position on an idea, this adds credibility to your claims. Beginners especially do not have much authority of their own, so showing that others are in agreement with you is a good idea. Friends add credibility, too. Look at their lives, experiences, the examples they set, or comments they have made that will help develop your points.

You now have a pretty meaty speech body, but this is not the end, it's the middle. This middle is sandwiched between an introduction and a conclusion. The introduction will be covered in detail in the following chapter. But first, the end.

6. The end

The conclusion of a speech is the ribbon on the package. Here everything that precedes is pulled together in simplicity and given to the audience to take home. This is the portion of your speech they will remember the most. Although writing the conclusion is near the end of the steps, some speakers find it helpful to write the conclusion first because it provides focus for the entire speech.

For the beginning speaker the conclusion is frequently the weakest part of the speech. The nervous speaker is so anxious to get offstage she blurts out, "That's it," grabs her notes, and runs. For this reason concluding remarks should be well-planned and practiced. "I guess," "That's it," "That's all I have," or "I hope you learned something," are limp excuses for escaping the audience's gaze. When you finish your speech you shouldn't be *hoping*; you should be *sure*. The ending should be strong and written in dynamic terminology. It is your last chance to make an impact on the audience.

In a writing class I learned an easy way to construct the beginning and ending paragraphs of an essay.[4] The same concept (with some modifications) applies to speech introductions and conclusions.

Diagram 3 is the visual picture of a conclusion, an inverted funnel. The first part of a speech's conclusion is narrow, beginning with a specific statement: the restatement of your theme. From this focussed remark the conclusion widens to broader aspects of the topic. The final statement tells the audience what you want them to remember, think,

---

4. Sheridan Baker, *The Practical Stylist* (New York: Crowell, 1962), pp. 18, 22.

feel, consider, or do about your theme. This closing remark is adapted to the type of speech you are giving and the particular audience. Between the specific and general in your conclusion are graduated degrees of memorable, succinct review information.

The functions of the conclusion are to signal the finish, restate the theme, review or illustrate main points, and give your listeners a "take away" statement.

The *signal* of the close of your speech makes the difference between the listeners' rapt attention and their sneaking out early to beat the rush. Employing deliberate delivery techniques is the best way to signal the impending close. These techniques will be discussed in chapter 9.

The concluding verbal signal should be a hint, not a declaration. Remarks such as "In conclusion," "In summary," and "In review," give the audience permission to stop listening. Avoid these.

I once sat in an audience of fifteen hundred women. When the speaker said, "In conclusion," fifteen hundred women picked up their purses, put on jackets, and started making plans for lunch with the persons next to them. *Be subtle.*

When the members of the audience sense you are about to close without your actually telling them so, they perk up.

Diagram 3

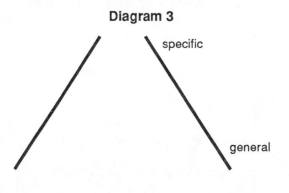

Signaling your finish with memorable remarks will accomplish this. Listeners will attend *if* the signal is given some fanfare. Build this signal with power-packed words: "An unforgettable woman . . .," "The crucial difference then is . . .," "Never, never, never . . .," "Ask not what your country can do for you, but. . . ." This is your last chance to hit your mark. Do it emphatically.

The *restatement* of your theme is just that: your theme repeated plainly. Hold back the frills. This second function of the conclusion will in itself serve as a conclusion alert. When you repeat your theme, the audience will sense things are winding down. This statement reinforces what was said in a variety of ways during the body of your speech and in the introduction. Repetition, although seemingly unnecessary to the speaker, increases audience retention. In the conclusion they hear the theme one last time clearly, simply, with nothing new added.

The third part of your conclusion — the *review* — when used creatively can be the most memorable. Poems, news clippings, witty sayings, or anecdotes can reiterate your point. One fellow who was soliciting kidney donors closed his speech with a gushing poem of gratitude written by a kidney recipient. It moved the audience without pushing them.

Using a quotation for a review reminds the audience that others agree with you, reinforcing your credibility.

If nothing memorable is available that captures the essence of your speech, then a brief review in your own words is in order. List your three or four points with a short statement of each. You may want to do this in addition to an illustration. They reinforce each other and can be used in any order or combination.

The *last remarks* of your speech serve as a directive. They tell us to remember, trust, pray, give. Often what you ask of the audience is not measurable or seen. Your effectiveness depends on well-chosen words of clarity. Out of such appeals slogans are born. "Only you can prevent forest fires," "Coke is it," or "You deserve a break today," are good examples of strong final statements that stick in the listener's mind.

If the audience has drifted into the Land of Nod during your speech, a strong conclusion will draw them back to your words. If they are attentive during the conclusion, and it is written correctly, they will hear your speech in capsule form in a way they will remember. Go out with a bang, not a whimper.

Work Sheet

1. Before proceeding to the next chapter, make a rough sketch of your speech. It does not need to be complete, but could simply include in abbreviated form ideas, anecdotes, and examples that you might include in each part of the speech body and conclusion. This is the rough draft for your *core* speech. In the following chapters you will see how part or all of this basic speech can be adapted to a variety of audiences and speaking situations.

2. Using what seem to be limited themes on your brainstorming list, develop short talks about them. Often what seems limited initially is packed with all sorts of potential.

5

Someone's Snoring, Lord!
Gaining and Maintaining
Audience Attention

Remove every obstacle out of the way of My people.

Isaiah 57:14

While I was speaking at a luncheon I noticed the head of an elderly lady gently bobbing. Looking around I realized she was not the only one. Two other women were also soundly asleep. I tried to comfort myself with my recollection of a retreat I once attended. The retreat speaker was in the middle of a lengthy prayer when a woman fifteen feet from her began snoring — loudly. At least my audience wasn't snoring, yet.

Gaining audience attention is our first responsibility as speakers. Most audiences will relinquish a moment of unearned attention before nodding off. Within this moment we must quickly cast the psychological hook that will catch the audience.[1] After all, we are to be fishers of men — and women.

A speaker rarely captures every fish in the sea. We know a few always slip through the net. Some people come only for the meal or to appease a pesky friend, but we can gain and maintain the attention of most.

One professional speaker described her technique this way:

> There I was, marching into the room with a lampshade on my head, a towel pinned around my shoulders, brandishing an umbrella like a baton, and singing a tune from *The Unsinkable Mollie Brown*.[2]

This is not a typical method of gaining audience attention, nor the only one that works. Many factors weave together to catch and hold the audience's attention: your knowledge about the audience, opening remarks, and delivery skills (discussed in chapter 9). In this chapter, we will explore attention getters to use in the written portion of your opening remarks and also focus on delivery skills which are used to gain audience attention.

H-e-e-e-r-r-r-e-s Julie!

Everything in the opening of your speech is geared toward gaining the audience's focus of attention, but the first factor happens before you speak. The words of the person introducing you dramatically affect the audience's anticipation of your speech.

1. Charles R. Gruner, *Plain Public Speaking* (New York: Macmillan, 1983), p. 115.
2. Sally Edwards Stone, "Writers Can Be Good Speakers," *The Christian Writer* (July 1985):30.

The introducer should establish your credibility by telling about your speaking experience, special training, or education. These facts combine to influence the audience's choice to listen. The members of the audience may be thoroughly impressed with the chairperson's comments about your ability. Then again, they may not.

An outstanding introduction will prime an audience to alertly anticipate the speaker. If you are fortunate enough to receive a good introduction, much of your initial work is completed for you. Unfortunately, those who introduce you do not always do their job adequately (see chapter 7).

The two creative ways you can deal with being introduced are preventive and reactive. To circumvent a disastrous start, approach the person assigned to your introduction before you are to speak. Give this person the list of your credentials and information about yourself you would like her to mention. This prevents embarrassing flattery as well as a flat underselling of your abilities. Be sure to clarify the pronunciation of your name and the organizations with which you are associated.

Even this ounce of prevention may not work. Your introduction may still be overdone, underdone, or give away your punch line. If the person who introduces you does not fulfill her job and establish your credibility, then it is up to you. It is a good idea to always be prepared for this possibility by having an alternate plan. It is easier to leave out extra material than to frantically add it as you go along.

Creating audience awareness of your credentials is not an exercise in ego strutting. Nothing drives people away from Christ faster than a puffed-up Christian. Rather, it is a modest answer to these listener questions: Why should I listen to you? What right do you have to talk about this topic?

Therefore, keep your opening remarks flexible enough to

accommodate mistakes by the person who has introduced you. If the introducer has overwhelmed the audience with a painfully detailed list of every degree, medal, and honor you've received, relieve them by showing you are human. One speaker asked her audience if they, like she, had shoveled their snow before coming to the luncheon that day.

To an overdone introduction you might comment, "Thank you for those kind words. You read them just the way I wrote them." Or, a more serious response I once heard was, "Those credentials are considered all loss compared with the highest credential of all: Jesus Christ living in me."

If your introduction has been deficient, weave small hints of your ability into your speech. You might offer the audience "A little bit more about myself...," "Last year when I spoke on this topic for...," or "I first became interested in...." This will let the audience know you have experience. But be careful not to overwhelm the audience with your qualifications, unless they are a highly educated or professional group. When weaving experience into your speech, strike that delicate balance between humility and ability.

Getting to Know You

At a luncheon, the speaker rushed in ten minutes before the program was to begin. "Oh, dear," she remarked while examining the audience. "I didn't realize this was a group of older women. My talk is on building self-esteem in small children. These women won't be interested in that!"

She was right.

In the last chapter we considered your topic choice from your viewpoint. Now let's consider it from the perspective of the listener. The audience is there for purely selfish reasons: to take from your speech what they can. If there is nothing of value for them they will lose interest. To prevent this you need to find out just what it is they want.

The speaker's task is to communicate relevant information that meets the audience's needs and interests. They cast the verdict on the fate of your speech. Every jury is composed of different individuals whom you must win over.

Just who is this audience?

Long before reaching the podium answer that question. Learn as much as possible about the group of people, their organization, and their community. This research prevents speaking disasters like the one just mentioned.

Here are some questions to answer about the audience before accepting a speaking engagement. What are the

1. Age, sex, educational and socio-economic levels?
2. Religious backgrounds or church affiliations?
3. Number expected to attend?
4. Purpose of the organization and situation in which you are to speak?

The more you can learn about these individuals and the bonds that hold them together, the better you can serve their needs. You may even decide you are not the appropriate speaker for this group, and that's all right. Maybe the Lord has someone better in mind for the job.

Gathering all this information is a precaution and is ideal, but it is not always possible. An experienced speaker can adapt to surprises, but the beginner may be taken aback. To the speaker on small children I suggested, "Why don't you remind them they all probably have grandchildren, nieces and nephews, or neighbor children whose parents could benefit from this information." She smoothly worked this remark into the opening of her speech. By her doing so the topic gained more relevance for the audience.

When you have gathered information about your audience, take a look at the information you gathered in working through chapter 3, and choose a topic most appropriate to their needs and interests. You can then tailor your speech to your audience.

The Funnel

The funnel illustrates the structure your beginning paragraphs should follow (diagram 4). Think of its function as being like that of any funnel: through it something is filled. This is the beginning into which you will pour your message.

The progression of a speech introduction is the opposite of the inverted funnel used for a conclusion. The introductory funnel starts with broad statements, then narrows to a specific statement of your theme. In between are several other necessary functions of an introduction.

If you have a flare for creativity, an unusual idea, go ahead and use it. In spite of the order you choose for the four items listed above, the attention getter must come within the first minute after the formalities, and all four ingredients must be included in your funnel.

These ingredients may appear to be too complex for a

Diagram 4

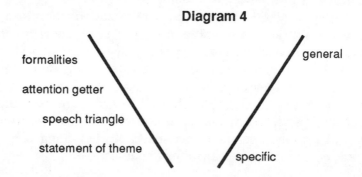

formalities

attention getter

speech triangle

statement of theme

general

specific

portion of your speech that should take no more than five percent of your speaking time. However, these functions are interrelated, and often one statement will serve two purposes. For instance, relating the topic to the audience may get their attention at the same time. Telling a story about yourself in order to gain attention may also establish your credibility. After reading the following descriptions of each function, you will see they are practically inseparable. Chapter 9 shows how delivery skills also serve in fulfilling these functions.

In the beginning — the formalities

Your first job is to clip through the formalities with grace and ease. The formalities are that initial section of your speech where you greet, thank, and acknowledge appropriate persons. Be sincere, but at an energetic rate. Showing your appreciation is essential, but the audience's anticipation will fade if you take too much time. Therefore, follow these simple rules for formalities: Be sincere; don't leave anyone out; build a bridge to the program that has preceded you; acknowledge the audience; be brief.

Everyone likes recognition. Baby-kissing politicians know this, but it isn't a matter of false flattery. Acknowledgment is a courtesy like a handshake or a smiley hello. Recognizing special officers, the person who introduced you, and important people or people who *think* they are important gains audience attention immediately.

Remark about earlier portions of the program, showing how it ties in (if it does) with you. Listen carefully to the program; you may hear something to which you can respond. Occasionally, a short anecdote about an experience related specifically to this gathering or one of its members may be appropriate.

The formalities section is best written in a few brief notes

while you are awaiting your turn at the podium. Just remember to follow the rules.

Attention Getters

The critical function in your funnel is gaining audience
attention. Communicating with an inattentive audience is
like trying to describe a new dress to your husband while
he is watching the World Series. If all the other functions in
your opening are fulfilled, but the audience is not glued to
your speech, you have failed. Nothing you say matters if the
audience isn't listening.

Capturing an audience's attention is more difficult today
than ever. The TV generation of our hurry-up world is overly
stimulated with rapidly changing scenes, sounds, and colors.
We have lost the ability to listen to anything bland and
slow moving. As speakers we must make our words and
actions competitive with the secular, our terminology colorful, and our pace lively. This may sound intimidating, but
a few carefully chosen words will often do the trick. Following are six categories of attention getters to perk up the
audience. Use them as springboards to your own creativity.

Opening line

"Before I begin I want to tell you who I am. I'm Corrie
ten Boom, and I'm a murderer." This arresting statement
was made by the woman whose Nazi concentration camp
experiences are the subject of *The Hiding Place*. You can be
sure her audience listened that day.

The first words of your speech are critical. They must be
the best. Too often the inexperienced speaker opens flatly
with "Good evening. Tonight my topic is ..." Opening remarks should point the audience toward the topic without
explicitly stating it until the end of the funnel. Strong re-

marks, unusual facts, powerful quotations, humor, and stimulating statistics related to your theme are possibilities. Reporting current research or news that causes an "I-didn't-know-that" response captivates the audience. We are fascinated with the extraordinary and drawn to the innovative. When you decide on a topic, begin collecting catchy information: later it will come in handy.

Choose opening lines in light of what you know about the audience, because these are the words that will determine whether or not the audience will listen. Most will stay; some will walk out, and others will sit politely while mentally making their grocery lists.

Whatever your opening remarks are, they should have starch and stand boldly, not hang from the podium like a wet noodle.

Storytelling

The most popular speakers and writers are those who can spin a yarn and make a fish story better. Telling a story is an effective way to open a talk. An audience is brought along easily by an entertaining story, because compared with a string of abstractions it makes for easy listening. My husband's favorite opening goes something like this:

> When Joe needed a speaker for tonight, he decided to call the best he could get. But the guy said, "No, I can't do it."
>
> Then Joe decided if he couldn't get the best speaker, he would get the best looking. So he called *him*, but he couldn't do it.
>
> So Joe thought if he couldn't get the best speaker or the best looking, he would ask the smartest. (pause)
>
> I just didn't have the heart to turn him down a third time.

Audience participation

"What is the most important thing that ever happened to you?" The speaker poses this rhetorical question to the audience without expecting a response other than thought. This type of attention getter actively draws the audience into your speech, provokes thought, and pushes out distractions.

The rhetorical question could be expanded into a quiz. This consists of a few short questions of which at least one should hit a resounding nerve within each audience member. It is that "That sounds like me" response that is most successful in captivating the audience.

Asking for a show of hands or for audience members to call out an answer are more active forms of audience involvement. One speaker had everyone count off by fours, had all the "fours" stand up, and asked, "Did you know that one in every four Americans will be touched by alcoholism in some way?" A physical response reinforces the thought process and solidifies your information. This was also a creative way to present a statistic.

Another way the audience can participate is by use of the imagination. Ask them to close their eyes and picture special surroundings, a situation, or a feeling. Take them vividly into that place, describing the smells, sounds, emotions, tastes. The more senses stimulated, the better.

Self-exposure

To speak is to be made vulnerable. When being honest about our struggles and failings we are often standing spiritually naked before strangers. As painful as this level of honesty is, it is here the Spirit of God can flow through us to touch lives.

Self-exposure is telling an audience something about ourselves they wouldn't otherwise know. This is done especially in testimonies when speakers reveal their lives before they knew Christ. Often this information is not flattering, something we would rather forget.

Disclosure does not mean telling all by dragging skeletal detail from our closets. One woman talked of uncontrollable rage she felt before she was a Christian, inferring she had been abusive. Her disclosure was not a confession of every black eye she might have inflicted, but a brief "I was awful and God forgave" statement made with a great deal of remorse. The audience forgave her, too.

When I feel the most exposed I am the most effective. Once, I spontaneously revealed my most embarrassing moment and immediately regretted it. Later, I found my admission had drawn respect from the audience instead of disgust.

Self-disclosure cuts through protective facades. Our human frailties are the "I've-been-there" link between speaker and audience.

Curiosity and suspense

"Today I'm going to share some information with you that could save your life." That's a real eye opener. We all want to live and we all will face death someday. This could introduce a speech about cardiopulmonary resuscitation, how to prevent hypothermia, or the salvation plan.

Waiting until the end of your introduction to reveal your topic is a method to keep the audience's attention. With the curiosity approach, the audience has a sense of direction but is unable to identify the topic specifically. Sales people use this, effectively building anticipation and excitement by withholding the old "bottom line." This very lack of information maintains the audience's interest.

The wondering keeps the audience mentally watching. One woman began her speech: "You've abused and neglected me. . . . My beauty has withered from lack of care." This was not a speech about wife abuse. Her words were spoken on behalf of Mother Earth. Her topic was pollution.

If you use this approach in your introduction, follow the standard format in which the focused topic statement is made at the end of the funnel. The difference in this approach is that the topic is not revealed by earlier comments in the introduction.

Humor

The ability to tickle the listener's funnybone is one of the speaker's greatest assets. Humor serves a multitude of purposes throughout a speech. I already mentioned in chapter 2 that humor can counter fear. It also warms the audience. Studies show and experience proves that if an audience anticipates humor they will listen better.

I can't help but think of Bill Cosby — just looking at him makes me smile. It is not because of his appearance, but because I know lurking just beneath the surface is a hilarious remark.

This does not mean if you begin your speech with humor the remainder must be riddled with jokes and wisecracks. It is just a pleasant beginning which nudges the audience in the direction of your theme.

Now that you've gained the audience's attention, you must keep it. Keep your finger on the audience's pulse. Although they may be a mixed group, they react with one personality. Energy and lethargy are equally contagious.

Audience response serves as a barometer for the speaker. Even negative reactions keep a speaker on track. Some audiences won't react negatively, but neither will they be enthusiastic. The best response to no response is to believe in your plan and enthusiastically carry it through.

If a lull overtakes the listeners at the wrong moment, ask

them another question, dazzle them with your wit, relate another story, but be sure to keep them awake.

The Speech Triangle

The speech triangle is much like the Bermuda triangle where so many planes are lost. The audience can be lost in this part of the introduction, too, if you're not careful. The triangle is best understood by seeing each side as being of equal length and force. Notice in diagram 5 the relationships between the speaker and the audience, the speaker and the topic, and the audience and the topic. They are interdependent; without one side, the triangle will collapse.

What do you have in common with this audience (speaker to audience)? Why are you the right person to talk about this topic, which to this point, although not explicitly stated, has been implied (speaker to topic)? Why does this group need this information (audience to topic)? A skilled introduction will answer these questions.

Relating the speaker to the audience

My favorite professor, Dr. Charles Van Riper, taught us a method of relating to a client in a therapy situation. He represented individuals by separate circles, functioning in their own spheres of experience and interest.

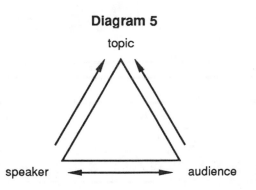

Diagram 5

In this new relationship the individuals merge into an area of commonality. The audience and speaker need the same relationship. As the speaker you must move to converge these separate worlds: find common footing, establish a honeymoon, be regular, be a friend, relate to where the audience lives.

Paul Harvey does this in his radio broadcast with the simple greeting "Fellow Americans." These two words say, "We are in this together." "Sisters in Christ," "Oneness enriched by our diversity," "We are here for mutual learning" are all effective statements that create an immediate sense of comraderie.

The audience likes to feel the speaker is "one of us." Words of commonality do this. So does poking fun at yourself or revealing your weaknesses. While leading a workshop a well-known Christian author said, "You'll have to excuse

Diagram 6

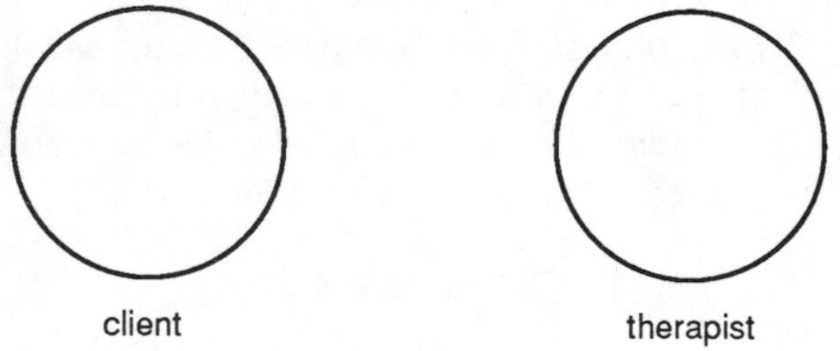

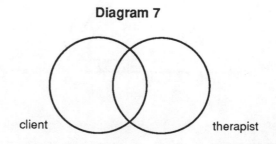

client   therapist

Diagram 7

client   therapist

me. I'm really disorganized today." The audience let out an immediate, sympathetic "awh." How delightfully ordinary. All we uncelebrated people also have those days!

Listeners want you to be a good speaker, knowledgeable on your topic, but not a superior person. And isn't that a big load off you?

Relating the speaker to the topic

Relating yourself to the topic is intricately related to establishing your credibility as a speaker. The introducer has told about your education, speaking experience, and other credentials, but you must relate yourself specifically to this topic. Some audiences will accept your competence based on the introduction. Others will weigh your comments and credentials heavily. Both base their conclusions on perceived knowledge.

Looking strictly at what you say, it is important to occasionally suggest your right to speak without overwhelming the audience. The best credential (besides being a Christian) is experience. If you have lived it you have a right to talk about it. A degree in nursing and three years teaching experience do not necessarily qualify you to speak about dealing with death. Someone who watched a family member die or was involved in a hospice program may be better qualified.

When establishing your relationship as a speaker to the topic, connect your remarks to an illustration. Use phrases such as "As my interest grew . . .," "Through this experience I learned . . .," "When I talked about it with . . .," "Because of my involvement I. . . ." When linked with an example that says, "I was there," you are a subtly established authority to speak on the topic. This process is an inoffensive demonstration of "I know what I'm talking about."

Relating the audience to the topic

After the commencement address, several students complained to me about the speaker. "She didn't say anything about us. All she talked about was her politics." This speaker was using the audience as a political stepping stone. Her interests and topics were related to another location and had little to do with our college and its graduates. Abusing your privileged platform is another way to lose your audience. The information you share must relate to the group hearing it, *and* you must point out this relationship.

Some speakers assume the audience understands the pertinence of the information to their lives. They don't. They need to be told. This is not insulting. A simple question such as "Do you see how this affects every one of us?" or "This could happen to you if you don't . . ." nudges the audience along your path of thinking.

Statement of theme

The theme or topic statement is the concluding function of the speech funnel. Usually before this point the audience anticipates the theme. Now make an explicit statement that tells the audience exactly what you intend to accomplish in your speech. The statement is focused, not vague, and often forecasts the main points as well. One of my topic statements sounded like this, "But how, you might be asking? How do I become God's superwoman? There are five characteristics of God's superwoman and I'd like to share those with you tonight." This concludes the introduction and alerts the audience that five points are about to follow, making listening easier.

We have explored the major functions of an introduction. You've studied the audience, humored them, impressed them with your brilliance, shown how important the topic is, and demonstrated that you're just one of the bunch. Whatever method you choose to mix these functions, just remember this: Your introduction should grasp the audience by the collar and say, "*This* you've got to hear."

Work Sheet

1. Using your core speech, imagine two different types of potential audiences to whom you might speak. Make the necessary changes in your introduction to adapt to each type of audience.
2. Read the beginnings of three articles or books. Study them to determine how the author captured your attention. Identify the topic statement.
3. Make a list of anecdotes from your life or someone else's, scenes from movies or books. After each, write the point it makes and save these ideas for illustrations in future speeches. They must show rather than tell.

6

A Word About Words
Setting the Tone and Choosing the Words in Your Speech

In the beginning was the Word, and the Word was with God, and the Word was God.

John 1:1

Words have power. God spoke the universe into being. The word spiraled off his golden tongue and ignited the brilliance of each star, the fire of Mars, and sent the moon spinning into its juxtaposition to the earth. Our words as well spin into the unknown universe within our listeners, setting fire to love gone dormant, piercing an inner sanctuary of hidden hurts, catching some falling star and igniting it with hope, rescuing personal planets on cataclysmic courses of self-destruction.

As speakers we must choose our words carefully, prayerfully, wisely. We are to handle truth accurately (see 2 Tim. 2:15). In his Epistle James tells us that those of us who teach carry greater judgment if we fail (James 3:1). Yet we cannot allow this to deter us from speaking on Christ's behalf. Neither should we choose timid words. Too often our words, like arrows short of their marks, drop into the orchestra pit without piercing the hearts of the audience. Good intentions must be coupled with prudent consideration and prayerful selection of our words.

Parlez-vous *Christianese*

During my first job as a speech therapist, I was asked to give a workshop for my fellow employees. Being the youngest and least educated on staff, I found this task intimidating. Thinking I would impress my co-workers, I loaded my lecture with terminology such as esophageal speech, echolalia, phonemic fears, and tongue-thrust swallow. Later, one the psychiatrists asked, "Would you mind explaining in terms I can understand exactly what you meant by all that?"

Speech pathology jargon was my problem. I assumed just because my audience was educated they were familiar with all the technical terms peculiar to my profession. Our culture is filled with such sublanguages, and unless you have studied a particular field, you will not understand its jargon. Christian disciples are no different.

Once, when teaching a Bible-study class, a Sunday school teacher asked me, "Just exactly what does 'saved' mean?" Most of us are too proud to admit when we are uncertain. Many of us are raised with religious lingo all around. Often it becomes an automatic part of our vocabulary without our having a firm understanding of its meaning. Then we throw these words at others and the problem spreads.

We Christians have our own timeworn form of esoteric

jargon. Liberal, fundamentalist, or charismatic, we talk in a sublanguage peculiar only to Christians "in the know." Newcomers to the faith are often driven away by such terms that threaten their spiritual self-esteem. Remember, even in a predominantly Christian audience there are the unchurched. They should not need a translator. Therefore, speak in a language anyone can understand. The idea is to communicate, not impress.

One of my pet peeves is Bible teachers who make such comments as, "Of course you all know the story about...." The person who doesn't know assumes everyone else does and she should, too. Meanwhile, seven others are secretly thinking the same thing. This creates feelings of inadequacy and causes the learner to lose confidence and interest. Do *you* know all the details of *every* Bible story and *everything* God said on *every* subject? Or, a verse can be read a hundred times and suddenly eyes are opened and it takes on a new meaning.

Words we choose should be understandable to all audience members. Christianity should not be an exclusive club where a password is needed for entrance. Furthermore, to be good speakers we do not need to become polysyllabic. Regular words do quite nicely. Words of understanding are understandable words. What language do you speak?

Listener guidelines

The audience needs signs, directions to point them along the way, much as drivers need to know when to stop or whether to pass or not. In writing, transitions subtly do this work. In speaking you need to be much more obvious with your transitions. The audience cannot see where you are going the way a reader can scan ahead on a page. An audience sees no indentations where new paragraphs begin nor extra spacing to indicate a change of topic. Words, specially chosen words, are the guides through your speech maze.

Listeners sometimes forget exactly which point you are covering, so repetitions and reminders mean they do not need to work hard to follow your train of thought. Vocal techniques such as pauses and changes of voice or pace aid in guiding the listener. These alone will not do the job unless coupled with words that indicate the direction your speech is taking. Here is a list of suggested transitions:

First of all . . .

Secondly . . .

My third point is . . .

In addition . . .

Another way to . . .

To begin . . .

Even more important is . . .

One example before I move on to my next point . . .

A final but most important method is . . .

One of the best illustrations is . . .

A good transition will not only forecast where you are going but recount where you have been:

I have just shown you one method; now . . .

The evidence I have just shown you . . .

That story demonstrates . . .

What we have seen here today, is . . .

Listener guidelines also alert the audience to what they should be doing:

For the next few moments, imagine . . .

Go with me to . . .

Stay with me for just a moment . . .

Picture yourself in . . .

Listener guidelines are the super glue that joins speech parts together and the audience to the speech. They can be used obviously and liberally.

Inoffensive

Not only should our words be easy to follow, they should be inoffensive. Solomon wrote: "The Preacher also taught the people knowledge; and he pondered, searched out and arranged many proverbs. The Preacher sought to find delightful words and to write words of truth correctly" (Eccles. 12:9, 10). Solomon was considered one of the wisest men in the Bible, and he was writing about himself. His delightful and carefully chosen words would not be offensive.

James tells us the tongue is a fire and the fire starts in hell. Destructive words — words that tear down instead of build up, words that criticize rather than praise, words that condemn rather than love — are not from God.

Words are murder weapons; they assassinate character, condemn ministries, and discredit God's people. Speakers must be cautious about setting fires with their tongues.

People are insulted by the strangest things. Even phrases like "God spoke to me" are reacted to defensively: "Well, I surely don't have that telephone line." "Sinners," "the lost," and "born again" repel many who resist salvation. "The Lord," suggests an intimacy with which many, including some

Christians, are uncomfortable. Terminology we use must be tempered to set well with each individual without compromising God's truth. The audience determines our choice of words as much as it influences our choice of topic.

Everyone brings a set of associations to a listening situation. Mother is synonymous with love to some, cruelty to others. Black could mean a race or a negative. Fire evokes images of a cozy winter day by the hearth or the rubble after a home is lost.

Speakers need to counter these unsolicited yet unavoidably evoked responses with clarification. When using terminology we must consider the listener's perspective. Precise wording with added explanation leaves the listener little room for wandering. Offense is often simply the result of misunderstanding.

If we are addressing a touchy issue, it must be handled with grace. A workshop leader was relating a scene from a novel about a preacher on his way to see a prostitute in order to demonstrate a point. "It's crude," she warned. "I hope you're not offended." This qualifier was a way of softening the information to follow, which was important to her point.

The sign I saw in a local restaurant puts it all in perspective:

Lord, make my words today
gracious and tender —
tomorrow I may have to eat them.

Happy Talkin'

Have you ever been around a negative person for long? I know one. With a nasal twang she drones on endlessly about bad news, prices, community problems, the weather, crime — complain, complain, complain. I have to avoid her at social functions or be guaranteed a headache.

Think of the people you enjoy being with. What are they like? Whom do others seem to gravitate toward? Who is the life of the party? It is the person who makes you feel good, the one who has something positive to say.

Humor is not a foxhole from life's harsh realities, but it is a cushion, some relief in the heat of battle, a time out. We all need to forget our problems for a little while; that's why we have vacations. Humor is a mental vacation, a laugh that jiggles our serious places and circulates life back to our hearts. It is no surprise to me that the most popular speakers are also the funniest.

Humor is one antidote to an emotionally laden speech. It prevents being bogged down in negatives by relieving the audience and the speaker. In the middle of my testimony, I stuck a plastic mustache under my nose and told how I used to dress as a man when driving my husband to the Army base at 4:30 A.M.

Humor is almost always appropriate, but it does not mean a string of jokes in the fashion of a standup comedian. It is a look, a pause in the right place, poking fun at yourself, relating an incident, or pointing out some incongruity.

Humor is a quality that unfortunately isn't always associated with Christians. We are perceived as "those" who are very serious about life and don't know how to have fun. Of course *we* know this isn't true. Our joy is different from that of the secular world's, and better. A display of a bright jovial spirit will do much to draw others to Christ.

I know a pastor who is full of wit. His hearty belly laugh can be heard wherever he goes. When he enters a room, people light up in anticipation of a good time. Those who rarely smile are often the first to respond. He is always the life of the party. His secret is his good sense of humor. This is what attracts so many to his church.

If we are to attract others to the body of Christ, we need to lighten their burdens with a little laughter.

Swamp talk

Many speakers are speakers because of the extraordinary experiences in their lives. Often these revolve around overcoming one tragedy or several. Too often, when relating her life story, the untrained speaker drowns the audience in depression in spite of her victory. The audience leaves feeling overwhelmed with life's injustices rather than energized by optimism. Because of increasing media coverage, most people are already painfully aware of the daily travesties of war, crime, and divorce. The audience needs relief.

I read about a man who in his escape from Russia found himself in the middle of a swamp. With each step he risked being pulled under, never to be found. But he persevered and reached the other side. What hope would there be for others had he given up and died in the swamp? Some speeches do that; they die in a swamp of depression.

Just yesterday I came away from a speaker feeling lethargic and depressed. Her problems seemed endless: poverty, abuse, divorces, dying children, physical and mental illness resulting in over a dozen years of psychiatric care. She dragged the audience through an hour of grueling detail.

"But," she announced brightly at the end, "the Lord got me through it all."

Several women later commented how depressing her speech had been. They were drowned by despair rather than helped, because the speaker never got out of the swamp.

A few months ealier I had listened to Tania Kauppila, author of *Survivor: A Woman's Search for Peace*. Her life was even more tragic. She suffered much of what the above-mentioned speaker had, and more: three years in a Nazi concentration camp, hunger during her entire youth, war, and loss of her entire family. After hearing her speak I left feeling like a conqueror, enthusiastic and ready to face the day, rather than looking for a place to hide from life.

The difference between these two speeches was the hope:despair ratio. Most of the first speech was spent dwelling on the negative. Most of the second was spent encouraging the audience and building us up. Mrs. Kauppila made a few remarks about her experiences in Russia, without elaboration.

The hope:despair ratio is critical in life as well as in the life of your speech. Public pity parties are taboo for the Christian speaker.

Florence Littauer, author and speaker, points out the only reason to tell about our suffering is to establish our credibility to speak on our topic.[1] We should not dwell on it and thereby pull the audience down. She is no stranger to suffering. Of the six hours she spoke at a weekend retreat, fifteen minutes she spent relating the story of the deaths of her two retarded sons; the other five hours and forty-five minutes of presentations she spent making us laugh while she made her point. This is true of most experienced Christian speakers.

A Christian counselor once said, "Self-pity is the most destructive force on earth." It certainly is the most destructive force in a speech. Often our problems have so colored our lives we cannot let them go. It is all right to cite the negative, but not to heap graphic details of our struggles onto the audience.

To prevent a weighted talk, practice on a listener who will

---

1. Florence Littauer, *Christian Leaders and Speakers Seminars* (Eugene, Oreg., 1983, audio cassettes).

be honest and assist you in creating an upbeat presentation. An objective friend can edit your speech better than you.

Don't leave the audience in the swamp. Eliminate as much negative as possible without damaging the effectiveness of your testimony, and *when in doubt leave it out*.

God's word

As speakers we should pray with the psalmist, "Let the words of my mouth . . . be acceptable in Thy sight" (Ps. 19:14). For our words to be acceptable we must be living in God's Word. Jesus instructed us: "If you abide in My word, *then* you are truly disciples of Mine" (John 8:31).

When the Word becomes part of us, it pulsates through our bodies, driving out negative poisons with positive nourishment. Flowing through us it invigorates our souls, sending life to the surface, healing deep-seated sores of unforgiveness, confusion, impatience. It tears loose festering wounds of waiting, worry, and want.[2]

Whatever is within us will color our language. Bitterness, fear, and other negative emotions will seep through our words and reach the audience unintentionally. We must drink in God's Word, constantly abiding there. If we are thinking on things that are good and pure (Phil. 4:8, 9), we will also speak these things. Being filled at his well gives us the living water that will cascade from our full vessels and quench our audience's thirst.

God's Word does not return void. When we speak it, souls begin churning. One woman talked about her lack of speaking credentials save one — Jesus Christ living within her. As she spoke his Word my internal universe was turned upside

2. Nancy I. Alford, "The Star," *Decision* (December 1985).

down and continued that way for three months. I was jarred from my safe place into the thrilling and frightening unseen path of faith. The Word of God is a causative force in our world. When we speak his truth, the speaking bears fruit.

"As the Spirit blows upon your listening spirit the Word of God finds expression in your words. He excites your language and style so that you communicate divine truth in the figures of human experience."[3]

The final word should be God's.

And other words

For Christians the spoken word is not just another pretty sound wave delighting the eardrums. Words build, destroy, rescue, motivate, devastate, praise, raise, and rebuke. Electric words jolt us into action, attack words bolt us to a cross, hollow words bore us.

With words we can captivate ("Are you ready for this one?"), recover ("If you could see my notes, you'd understand why I can't read them"), kill ("You stupid fool"), devastate ("You're not going to wear *that*"), or lead people astray ("God is dead," "Heil Hitler").

Words misinform: "Because I'm a Christian God kept me from that car accident."

"Do you mean if I become a Christian I won't have car accidents?"

"That's right!"

Words betray ("And do you know what so-and-so said?"), heal ("I love you"), alienate ("All Catholics are going to hell"), and draw together ("Brothers and sisters in Christ").

Words are positive ("You can if you think you can!"[4] "Tough

3. Wallace Alcorm, "Inspiration — Be Ready for It," *Decision* (February 1985):34.

4. Norman Vincent Peale, *You Can If You Think You Can* (New York: Fawcett, 1976).

times never last, but tough people do"[5]) or negative ("You'll never make it," "That's impossible").

The original Word was flesh and lived among us. We crucified him. The Word must now live within our flesh, and be articulated to the world accurately. "Set a guard O LORD, over my mouth: keep watch over the door of my lips" (Ps. 141:3).

Work Sheet

1. Scan your core speech for words that might be misunderstood, offensive, or negative. Replace them with better choices. Also monitor your daily conversation for these words. You may find them popping out uninvited.
2. Scan your speech for transitions. Where they are lacking, add some from the list in this chapter or create your own.
3. Check your speech for statements that are inconsistent with Scripture. Correct these thoughts.
4. To expand your vocabulary, begin listing words you hear or read that are colorful, positive, and different. Look them up in a dictionary and gradually work them into your vocabulary.

5. Robert H. Schuller, *Tough Times Never Last, But Tough People Do!* (New York: Bantam, 1983).

7

Special-situation Speeches
Writing the Short Speech

When there are many words, transgression is unavoidable, but he who restrains his lips is wise.

Proverbs 10:19

Special-situation speeches are simply speeches given for a special occasion or specific purpose. All such speeches are brief and draw attention to someone or something rather than to you. Just as a lengthy speech, the special speech requires an introduction, body, and conclusion. Beyond these commonalities each calls for its own particular guidelines different from the others.

Because these speeches are always brief, effort is usually proportionate. The short speech, however, needs as careful and thorough preparation as a lengthy talk.

There is a blessing in brevity. The time boundaries prevent careless rambling into superfluous fluff; you need to get right to the point in the time you have. These limits, however, are not always respected. As a result, neither is the speaker. If you get a reputation for long windedness, no one will invite a repeat performance.

The length of time given to a special speech is one of balance. You need not spend fifteen minutes introducing someone giving a twenty-minute speech, thirty minutes announcing the upcoming barbeque, or forty-five minutes accepting an award. Common sense is the rule of thumb. Spend no more time than you need to get the facts and your point across.

The Ten Commandments contain fewer than three hundred words. The Gettysburg Address is only 266 words.[1] It took two minutes to deliver.[2] Each is about one typewritten page. A few words can be power-packed when carefully chosen.

Making announcements

An announcement is hardly the main feature of any function. It is the briefest of special speeches and therefore must get right to the point by packing much into few words. Because of its brevity an announcement needs to be well-planned, succinct, and filled with enthusiasm.

For a successful announcement Florence Littauer suggests the following:

> The simple solution for clear announcements is to follow the "Five Journalistic W's: Who, What, When, Where, and Why.
>
> Who is sponsoring the activity?
> What is its plan and purpose?
> When is it being held?

1. Stan and Pam Campbell, "The Bent Commandments," *Power for Living* (October 21, 1984):8.

2. Philip B. Kunhardt, "Abe Lincoln's Failure," *Reader's Digest* (November 1983):199.

Where will it be?
Why is it important to attend?[3]

Be sure to get names right, and have all the information *before* making the announcement. Don't stop in the middle to ask for details from the chairman who is sitting in the audience. However, if you have failed to do your homework, it is better to get clarification this way than give out misinformation.

It is best to get right to the point when making announcements. A long introduction is unnecessary. The audience does not want to be entertained. They just want the facts.

Have you ever noticed how certain people are able to get volunteers to teach Bible school, bake cookies, and make bazaar gifts? The sixth ingredient to a successful announcement is enthusiasm, which should be generously sprinkled over the five w's! If you are not excited about the upcoming event, who will be?

A personal endorsement is always important. If you cannot say that you will be there, don't expect others to attend. Tell them how much fun it will be, how informative, exciting, inspirational, or tax deductible! Get those attractive terms up front where they will work for you.

I remember an announcement about a "fantastic" man who would be sharing his "incredible" testimony and "marvelous" music at a church. He was billed with such exuberance and positive terms I could hardly wait to hear him. Throughout the program I continued to wait for the "fantastic" and "marvelous." I finally realized I'd been had. I had fallen for an incredibly convincing announcement about a terribly boring person.

3. Florence Littauer, *It Takes So Little to Be Above Average* (Eugene, Oreg.: Harvest House, 1983), p. 116.

Being a worship or program leader

Another speaking occasion which may arise is that of leading a church service or special program. This involves not only speaking but oral interpretation skills as well. The responsibilities may vary with different churches or organizations, but usually include all or some of the following: announcements, introductions (covered later in this chapter), guiding the service, prayer, and Scripture reading.

To begin you must draw the group's attention to the program. During a church service this is usually not a problem, but in other settings you may have to regulate the people as well as the program. Be sure to invite the audience back to their seats and wait for their attention before continuing. The audience may be finishing a meal, returning from a coffee break, or wandering in from another workshop. Take charge, creating an atmosphere of receptivity and attentiveness.

You set the tone for what follows. Be pleasant and personable when such are called for (which is most of the time) or serious and professional on more formal occasions. Know the agenda in advance, and check with others to be sure they know when and how to participate. Be flexible enough to accommodate their mistakes. You are the cohesiveness, the bonding factor in the program. If someone gets out of order or misses an item in the bulletin, creatively add it.

Public prayer should be delivered with feeling. You may be more comfortable with one you have written word for word in advance, but it is better to have ideas of the prayer's content that you deliver naturally and do not read. This allows for spontaneous additions and special requests. Thinking of this as time with God rather than a performance is the key. Deliver the prayer to God sincerely. He is the most important listener.

Scripture reading may also be part of your role as leader. With the Bible containing so many unusual names and places, its passages should be studied in advance. Check pronounciation with your pastor before stumbling over a word publicly. The Word of God is special and should be presented that way, not read like the morning newspaper. First be sure you understand the selection from Scripture you are reading. In order to breathe life into it, keep the significant message of the verse or chapter in mind as you read. Put inflection where the writer would had he spoken the words rather than written them.

I remember one fellow who flatly read, "Praise the Lord," (audible sigh) "Oh Praise Him . . ." (another sigh) and on he droned. This was a psalm full of the spirit of worshiping God, an exciting privilege, but the leader did not communicate this attitude.

Regardless of the setting, the keys to success in this multifaceted role are preparation, alertness, and flexibility. To guide any program successfully, know what to do and when to do it. This keeps it flowing, uninterrupted by awkward pauses.

Presenting awards

Whether for the recipient or the giver, awards involve speech making. Both must plan and execute their words briefly and appropriately.

The award giver's speech must include the recipient's role and reason for being recognized and an anecdote or example that demonstrates her character or outstanding qualities. Follow this by stating on whose behalf you are presenting the award, and directly express your appreciation to that person or organization.

I once watched Ed McMahon receive an award on television. The man giving it stared at the statue as if he were reading its lips. When presenting an award, look at the recipient; she is where all attention should be focussed.

Take time to put some thoughts on paper. Even though this is a short speech, a few notes are fine to use. But even then, success is not guaranteed.

I once was selected to give a spur-of-the-moment presentation. I made a brief outline, first giving a little background about the people receiving the awards, complimented them on how hard they had worked, and thanked them by name while two girls presented them with bouquets. It went perfectly, I thought. Then my daughter said, "Mom, her name is Ann Beamer, not Bremer!"

Even though I had written out her name, I still didn't get it correct. Make notes and then use them.

Receiving a gift or award

We have all squirmed in our seats while some embarrassed recipient of an award stands with his jaw unhinged and finally says thank you and nothing more. If you have been nominated for an award or think there is the slightest possibility that a group may want to publicly display appreciation to you, be prepared. There is nothing egotistical about privately putting a few words together *just in case* you need to use them. But don't get carried away. We have all suffered through listening to a person enamored with the microphone and after pecking at it a few times finally grabs it and struts across stage. She then runs on, giving a personal history of the details that brought her to this point of achievement thirty-five years later. As my daughter would say, "Deeeesgusting."

Besides finding a creative way of saying thank you, in your moment of glory don't overlook those who contributed to your success. Although the audience doesn't really care about this show of appreciation, those you mention will. Be sure to do it.

A group that loves you enough to give you an award is likely to tolerate even the sloppiest thank-you speech, as long as it is short. Be thoughtful, appreciative, but brief.

An athlete once said he couldn't enjoy receiving the Sullivan Award because he knew he had to give an acceptance speech. Fear of such situations is a joy robber. Prepare. It will prevent turning an honor into a horror.

Delivering the impromptus

"Tonight we have a special person in our midst. Sally Sorry has been one of our avid behind-the-scenes supporters. Without her help our project would not have been possible. Sally, would you mind coming up and sharing a few words with the group?"

Sooner or later it will happen to you. When you least expect it, your name will be called from the podium. You will stumble forward in a fog of disbelief, desperately trying to pull some meaningful words from your dazed mind.

The impromptu is a spur-of-the-moment speech, but you can still be prepared. The best way is to recognize the potential of being called on whenever you are in a group. As you sit at a meeting, banquet, or even in church ask yourself why you might be asked to speak.

Dale Carnegie recommends three sources of potential information for the person caught in an impromptu situation (they are available to you, however, only if you have been an alert listener):

1. The audience — talk about the listeners.
2. The occasion — why are these people here?
3. Another speaker — mention something specific he said.[4]

4. Dale Carnegie, *The Quick and Easy Way to Effective Speaking* (New York. Pocket Books, 1962), pp. 152–53.

Anything said during the program has potential use in your impromptu. Briefly outline in your mind some appropriate remarks. Then relax and enjoy yourself, but pay attention.

Putting together thoughts on the spot demands quick thinking and presence of mind. Before arriving in such a perilous situation, practice impromptu thinking at home. Have your husband give you a topic. Think about it for one minute, then talk about it for one minute. This exercises those mental muscles that assist you in thinking on your feet when you are under pressure. When your turn comes publicly, it will be easier to maintain your presence of mind.

Jane was to give a presentation following that of her husband. They both stood at the podium while he spoke. She then opened her notebook with obvious shock as her husband wrapped up his talk. Sensing a warm and sympathetic audience she related how, as she raced from her home, she grabbed her address book instead of her speech notebook. The audience had a good laugh, and she went on to give a fine speech.

As Christians we are thrust into many impromptu speaking situations. They are usually not in an auditorium, but at a friend's house, the hospital, or the Little League game. Evangelistic opportunities present themselves daily. We need tucked in our minds mini-speeches, responses Peter admonished us to give to those who question us (see 1 Peter 3:15). Mentally addressing the issues with which we may be confronted readies us to answer. This forethought changes an uncertain impromptu attempt at evangelism into a sure thing.

One day a tearful friend confronted me after relating a traumatic experience. "What difference does it make, being a Christian?" We need to be ready with answers for these situations. When you meet a stranger or friend, do you know what to say in defense of your faith?

I was able to answer my friend because I had once asked the same question from my own pit of despair. But what if I hadn't? We need to explore these issues before being put on the spot. Even when giving a speech you may be questioned from the audience, and you need some forethought from which to pull your responses.

To be ready for life's little impromptus, write out your thoughts on a number of issues. Start with a mini-version of your testimony and a working knowledge of how to lead someone to Christ. You never know when someone may challenge your faith or ask for help. Your impromptu response to someone desperately searching for hope may be the most important speech you'll ever give.

Giving an introduction

For every five million speeches given annually five million introductions are made. Additionally, musicians, chairmen, and guests are introduced, making this special-situation speech a frequent one. Introducing someone is a serious responsibility and should be planned and delivered with great care. It can so influence an audience that they will listen even if the speaker lacks competence. What you say or neglect to say can make or break that person's ability to stand before an audience.

One professional vocalist was to sing for a PTA luncheon. The woman introducing her was a close, long-time friend. She carried on about her marvelous singing and accomplishments for too long. The vocalist became unglued by the flood of compliments and left in tearful humiliation.

Then there is the opposite extreme: "And now we will hear from someone who needs no introduction." There is no such animal! Even professional speakers and performers need to hear a few complimentary words to help boost them from the wings to center stage. This situation unfairly leaves the speaker with the embarrassing task of tooting her own horn as modestly as possible — which isn't very easy!

The proper introduction accomplishes three things:

1. Puts the speaker at ease.
2. Establishes the speaker's credibility.
3. Creates audience interest.

In order to succeed in fulfilling these responsibilities you should interview the guest well in advance of the speaking engagement. Begin by asking the speaker what she would like the audience to know about herself. An experienced speaker will know what credits and experience are worthy of mention. Continue by inquiring about her education, awards, family, current involvements, or work. Gather more information than you need. It is easier to edit than pad a speech.

Once you have gathered information, check it with the speaker for accuracy and use. You may have information she would not like mentioned. Respect the speaker's confidence. Her approval is important if she is to feel comfortable.

Most importantly, get her name right! If it is difficult to pronounce, then practice it. Mispronouncing their name is an insult to most people. It also signals to the audience you didn't consider this person important enough to do your job correctly.

Now that you have done your research, cast the information into the format listed below. Keep in mind the three points just mentioned. The length of an introductory speech varies with the length of the speech to follow. Four minutes would be the maximum length for any introduction, varying downward to a minimum of thirty seconds.

Follow these four steps when introducing a speaker:

1. Greet the audience and introduce yourself if no one has done so. The speaker's name and title may be mentioned next or at any point during the rest of the introduction. It is typically mentioned here. With speakers who are well known to the audience, the name may be withheld until the end of step 4.
2. Relate the speaker's qualifications. This includes education, speaking experience, accomplishments, and those things which uniquely qualify her to speak on her topic. Begin by building up — in positive terms and an enthusiastic voice — the person about to speak. Building audience anticipation is the kindest gift you can give the speaker.
3. Paint a personality picture. Glean from your interview with the speaker some glints or feelings about her personality, spirit, attitudes, etc. She may have related an anecdote about herself that you could pass on. The audience should feel the speaker is a real person, not some ominous star in the limelight, but ordinary and likable in many ways. I heard one man introduced by a friend as "a ray of sunshine in a fog alert." This gave an immediate feeling that we would like the speaker.
4. End with a positive and enthusiastic endorsement of the speaker. The entire introduction should have this tone, but especially the final note. You are the cheerleader. Tell the audience how much you are looking forward to hearing this person. The air should be charged with anticipation when you finish.

Fund raising

Fund raising is a special form of persuasive speaking. It is not always a brief speech, but is brief more often than not. Whether long or short, the pattern remains the same, and usually the situation in which the speech is given is designated for this purpose.

Before asking for money, tell the audience the functions of your organization or nature of your project. Most people want to be informed about what is being done before they are willing to invest in it.

The worth of the project must also be demonstrated. This is done by showing results. Statistics of the number of commitments made, people fed, or lives helped are proof the organization is accomplishing something.

Testimonials are another way to show an organization's worth. A letter from someone affected by your work is probably the most persuasive. Often hearing about one real person means more to an audience than impersonal numbers. The alternative would be to relate individual experiences second hand. Tell about success situations that were reported to you. Whatever form it takes, the audience needs evidence. If you can use all three types, then by all means do so.

People are becoming more and more suspicious about how their money is being spent. My husband helped spearhead a youth soccer program in our community that has two fund raisers a year. People ask where "all that money" is going, as though it were going into the pockets of the organizers. We are accountable to contributors. This can be accomplished by publishing a financial statement, breaking down the distribution of a dollar, or by indicating the total cost of a specific project or item.

Finally, when actually asking for funds, relate cost factors to where the potential donors live. "If you give up one meal a week, it will pay for. . . ." Be specific and direct in what you would like them to give. For instance: "If each person here tonight gave $50 it would finance our mission work for an entire year." Facts must accompany your appeal. Emotion alone is a short-run motivator.

One speaker, whose only income is donations, explained her insights about givers. She said some have the gift of giving, but this money cannot be coerced from them. Guilt, desperate appeals, and pressure tactics do not motivate these special people. The Holy Spirit does. Just as in showing the way to salvation, *we* do not convert people, neither do we *make* people give their money. The giving is not an issue you can force. You cannot know the heart of an audience nor whom God has touched with the spirit of giving. You are the instrument through which others are made aware of the needs. That is the end of your job.

Work Sheet

1. Write an introduction to yourself the way you would like to hear it done. Don't be modest!
2. Write your response to an award or recognition that you would like to win someday. You never know, it just might happen when you are least expecting it.
3. Exercise your mental muscles with a partner. Each write topics on separate cards. Draw from each other's stacks of cards, taking one minute to think about the topic and one minute to talk about it.

8

Witnessing
Writing Speeches to Inform and Persuade

Let your speech always be with grace, seasoned, as it were, with salt, so that you may know how you should respond to each person.

Colossians 4:6

Whithat is a witness, evangelist, preacher, teacher? These roles seem awesome to us. We hold back, feel unqualified, yet we are obligated as Christians to get the bushel basket off our light, the salt out of our shaker. In terms of public speaking, these roles are much the same. Women preach the word.

Evangelistic opportunities for women present themselves nationwide. Usually, public speaking situations in which Christian women find themselves are designed for just that: Christian women to tell about their faith. Women's groups exist within every church. Interdenominational organizations for women have developed and are flourishing. Other opportunities exist through organizations, Bible-study programs, and in-home groups. Wherever you reach, the needs are great.

One woman was so excited about her new faith she put an advertisement in the paper for a Bible study group. Fifty women came from ten different churches and traveled as far as thirty-five miles to the study she led. God will use you if you are available.

The first thing to remember about witnessing is that God does not call you to wander outside your realm of experience. He may ask you to stretch yourself through Bible reading and prayer, but he won't ask you to talk about Christian bricklaying if you are not a mason. Jesus said, "We speak that which we know, and bear witness of that which we have seen" (John 3:11). That's all he asks.

What have you seen? What do you know? What are you learning? These are the questions you answered in chapter 3. Take another look. As Becky Pippert says in her book on evangelism, "Our message is not that we have it all together. Our message is that we know the One who does!"[1] Spiritual graduate school is not a requirement for witnessing.

Witnessing is informative and persuasive, and sometimes both. Christian workshops and conferences, Bible studies, teaching, preaching, and giving testimonies combine these two basic speech types: to inform and to persuade.

The Speech To Inform

Informative speaking is simply giving information. The intent is not to bring about change, although this may result

1. Rebecca M. Pippert, *Out of the Saltshaker and into the World* (Downers Grove, Ill.:Inter-Varsity, 1979), p. 121.

indirectly. Telling how to do a craft, giving information about a club or organization, announcing church plans for expansion, teaching Sunday school, giving your testimony are examples of informative speaking.

A speech to inform is telling. It is sharing information about yourself, an issue, idea, or thing; the imparting of the new or the old in a new way. Chapter 4 covered the format for this and any other type of speech: an introduction, body containing a three- to five-point outline, and a conclusion.

Although the intent of informing is not necessarily to bring about change, for the Christian there is no speaking without persuading. We witness, lead, and teach with one underlying purpose in mind: to draw others closer to Christ. Whenever we speak, it is to glorify God. Therefore, we will discuss the preparation of your testimony in detail.

Your testimony

Preparing your story can be the most exciting venture of your spiritual life. As I explored my walk with God my faith was renewed by the fresh reminders of all he had done for me. How like us to forget the joy after the moment has passed.

There are many types of informative speeches, but giving your testimony is the most common type of speech made by Christian women. Although you can testify about any time in your life when God can be seen working, a testimony is usually considered a talk about the events surrounding your conversion. The structure of your testimony is chronological: your life before you were a Christian, the circumstances that brought you to the point of commitment, and the changes in your life after your decision. I have never heard a testimony given any other way. You are, after all, first a nonchristian and then a Christian, and you sometimes fluctuate back and forth before arriving at a point of solid commitment. Either way, there is a sequence to these events. The progression toward God (including a little backsliding) is the essence of a testimony.

The objective of the testimony is not a sentimental journey like showing home movies of your first attempt at roller skating. Rather, it is a personal illustration of the change God brought to your life *so that* others will want what you now have. That is the reason to give it, not to entertain a group for the afternoon.

The structure and content of your testimony is the same regardless of the time in which you are alotted to give it, whether three minutes or an hour. The only variable is the amount of detail and examples used and possibly the number of points made. In using chapter 3 you looked at your life. It is now time to draw from those notes the information pertinent to your testimony.

Painting a before-salvation picture of yourself is an essential ingredient when giving your testimony. I was once a spoiled brat living a joyless life. Establishing this during my testimony is important to my contrasting life as a Christian. The audience needs to see how you were, flaws and all, before you came to Christ. Heaven is not occupied by perfect people. It is filled with murderers like Paul and those who denied Christ as Peter did. Admitting your mistakes is a big relief to the audience. It lets them know God does not call the perfect but the flawed to him.

When personal information is given sincerely, the audience is moved. Nothing is more captivating than to hear from a former drug addict or alcoholic. I've listened to such confessions in a room where not a breath could be heard. Keep in mind, though, you do not need to give all the details. Reveal only what is necessary to your story without embarrassing yourself or anyone else.

Your conversion is the transition between the old life and

the new. Often a series of events lead like stepping-stones to your commitment. What brought you to the turn in the road? Were you on a downhill spiral, did you sense something was missing in your life, or was everything rosy? Was there a Christian who had a profound influence? What made you see the unfilled need in your life? For me life seemed okay until I "accidentally" watched the 700 Club TV show. I soon started watching it regularly. I saw the joy in the lives of those Christians, and I wanted it, too.

At the point of explaining your conversion, give the why and the how. It is important to demonstrate the process clearly enough for others to know how they can make a commitment, too. In relating your experience don't be afraid of ordinariness. Most can identify with that better than with intense, spiritual experiences, although these are certainly valid as well.

I simply prayed with the persons on TV but didn't feel like anything had happened within me. I wondered if I was really a Christian. I had many questions a TV couldn't answer, so I prayed one thing — that God would send a Christian into my life who could answer my questions. Six months later after moving to another city I received a phone call. "I've picked your name at random out of the phone book to answer some questions for a survey for Campus Crusade for Christ. Could I come over?" And so my prayer and my questions were answered.

What difference did it all make? You had your life before you chose Christ; how is life better now? We need to be honest and not hand the audience a rose without the thorns. We know tragedy befalls all of us in spite of our faith. For me the major trials and griefs came after I was a Christian, but so did something else — the joy I was seeking. The difference for Christians is in the getting up again, the going on with the Comforter. And of course, the difference is eternal.

What is new? What has changed? How has this new relationship with Christ impacted your life? The audience needs to know.

These three points — the before, the conversion, and the after — should take approximately equal time in your speech. Every life is unique, resulting in some variation in time, but don't spend twenty minutes telling how wretched your past was and then pronounce, "But God saved me and I've lived happily ever after." A balance must be struck.

The above three-point outline is to be sandwiched between an introduction and a conclusion, the functions of which are covered in chapters 3 and 4.

With the conclusion of a testimony it is important to also pray with the audience, offering them the opportunity to know Christ. Pray with them, and make yourself available for questions. How inappropriate it would be to proclaim all he has meant to you, the joy he has brought to your life, and then not help others find it for themselves.

The Speech to Persuade

Persuasion is selling. It is an informative speech plus an intentional attempt to bring about some type of change in the thought, word, or deed of the listener. Informing is part of this type of speech, because the audience must be educated about the topic before they can accept it or change their present position.

You have probably already given a persuasive speech without realizing it. Soliciting members for an organization, inviting someone to a prayer meeting, asking your husband for a dishwasher or your boss for a raise are all persuasive speeches. Some people have no difficulty making these requests. They have convincing qualities impossible to dissect from their personalities. Still, all persuasion follows specific principles and steps anyone can learn.

Persuasion is selling, whether it is to sell an item, belief, value, attitude, or new way of life. Persuasion is a multi-faceted creature. It is dependent on situation dynamics, the mind of the targeted audience, and you the persuader. You can exercise varying amounts of control over these factors when you prepare your words with an understanding of the following principles of persuasion.

Be positive

Persuasion requires much more energy than any other speech. To convince you must enthuse, encourage, inspire, excite, and have enough energy to carry the audience along on your coattails. If you believe without reservation in what you are promoting, positive emotion will be a natural result. Positive emotion moves mountains and stubborn people. You have probably had a salesman take you by storm, and you wound up being the proud owner of a new vacuum cleaner you didn't need. This kind of persuasion results from a whirlwind of enthusiasm and confidence.

On woman requesting volunteers for the post-Christmas cleanup said blandly with a sigh, "It's the same old bunch every year." Would you want to help this woman? Guilt is an inappropriate and poor motivator. It repels the very people you want to respond.

Bathe your request in positive terms. One man needed volunteers to mow the church lawn. First he told how "Doc" had been doing it for sixty-seven years. This obvious exaggeration created a little chuckle. He went on to explain how much "fun" it was to use the riding lawn mower and how "easy" that made it to finish in a "short" period of time. I was ready to sign up!

Being positive means being aware of the drawbacks as well. Everything has its good and bad side. Present the good first. When Jesus said to Peter, "Follow me," he didn't add in the same breath, "so that you can be martyred for me after I'm crucified." How appealing would that be to a some-day Christian? It wasn't until the end of his ministry that Jesus told Peter how he would die. Then Peter was better prepared for this information. Some discernment and question asking will tell you whether or not your audience is ready for milk or meat (Heb. 5: 12–14).

To point out the negative aspects of an idea you are trying to sell is counterproductive unless you couple it with an explanation. People usually have enough of their own arguments against change and new ideas without the speaker fueling their resistance. You can anticipate the audience's objections by thinking like the audience and asking yourself how they might argue against your point. Then build a rebuttal into your speech. This takes away their excuses.

Be discreet

As a general rule for the public speaker, persuasion does not mean force. It is the art of gently moving, a breeze across the mind, not a tornado. Proverbs tells us, "A soft tongue breaks the bone" (25:15). What an unlikely concept to enter the earthly mind! When we think of the stubborn man we tend to respond with stubborn determination. When we are pushed we respond with resistance.

If someone approached you with his hand out and said, "Gimme a hundred bucks," you would resist. If he at least said, "Hello, how are you?" you would feel better toward him. If he first took the time to have a conversation and explain why he needed the money, then you might even be willing to give it.

Discretion does not mean sneaky. Remain honest, but

ease into your point of difference with the audience. First establish points of agreement, rapport, what you have in common. Gradually build toward the change, and the positive atmosphere you create will have a more lasting effect.

It takes all kinds to win all kinds. Your style of persuasion must be consistent with your personality. It will appeal to some, but it should appeal to most. When Jesus led Peter out to a fishing spot, he said, "Put down your nets," not "Grab those suckers around the throat and give a good squeeze." Many well-intentioned zealots go for the jugular and, amazingly, succeed. But their results soon fade, because they neglect to build a firm foundation. Often leaders do this by using guilt. They tend to squeeze the very joy out of us in order to expose our sinfulness. Then, stripped of all that is good within us, we are persuaded.

There are times when a show of righteous indignation is appropriate. Jesus usually displayed this when addressing the Pharisees. There is a correct time to take a stand, as when Jesus threw the money changers out of the temple. These times should be carefully chosen.

Our community has an annual gathering of women from all churches in the county on the World Day of Prayer. This is a day of unity, the banding together of women with diversified Christian ideologies for the common purpose of prayer. One year the lovely Catholic ladies were blasted out of their pews by one of the speakers. Clearly insensitive to the spirit of the day, she took advantage of her platform to, as she told me later, "let them have it" on the issue of birth control. The service ended with insulted participants, an embarrassed host church, but a smugly satisfied speaker.

Be specific and simple

Before you begin your speech, be sure it is clear in your own mind what you want this audience to do. Be small in your expectations; this isn't going to be a giant spiritual leap for mankind. Once you know *what* you would have them do, clarify *how* they are to do it. Write the answers to these two questions and build your speech around them.

Be direct in what you want your audience to do or change. God-talk is not specific. Referring to being "cleansed by the blood" sounds barbaric to those lacking biblical understanding. Put your directives in plain, everyday language with detailed instructions.

If you tell your audience to get closer to God, will they know how? Such a vague and abstract request leaves lots of room for misinterpretation. Specify: "Set aside a half hour a day to read one chapter in your Bible, beginning with the Gospel of John." When you relate the spiritual coupled with real life examples, it is more easily understood.

Minimizing the effort and giving specific instructions to your audience enhances the chance for success. One woman soliciting funds for research for childhood cancer succeeded. After telling of the death of her twin sister to cancer at age eight, she asked each of us to put our hands in our pockets or purses and paused, giving us an opportunity to do so. "Most of you have some loose change. The next time you see a canister near the cash register in the store, reach into your pocket and donate that change. It's only a little bit, but it could make a big difference." Her call to action was simple. Involving our kinesthetic sense by having us reach for and feel the change helped firmly plant that thought in our memories. It's been several years, and I haven't forgotten.

One well-known author, speaker and magazine editor knew how to minimize the effort when soliciting subscriptions to his publication. After he spoke to a few thousand businessmen and businesswomen, someone followed him to the podium to promote his magazine with a persuasive speech about its worth. Men then went to the end of each row of seats and passed down subscription forms that were collected by someone at the other end. No money required; you could fill in your credit card number. He made it very simple to say yes.

Ignorant and hostile

The best philosophy to use when approaching any audience is to consider them potentially ignorant and hostile. Before you take offense, let me explain. An ignorant person is not stupid. Ignorance is a lack of information on a topic. For instance, I am ignorant about calculus because I have never studied it; that does not mean I am incapable of learning about it.

The audience's ignorance does not mean you should talk down to them. Rather, challenge and stretch them, but not too much. You are giving new information to help them grow. Keep it within their reach.

If you also write your speech with a hostile audience in mind, you are anticipating objections and eliminating them before they actually occur. Imagine a group actively resistant to your speech and boldly expressing that opposition. Scan your speech for words that are offensive or could be misinterpreted.

Next, coat your speech with genuine kindness, love, and concern. It is difficult for a listener to be angry with someone who cares. When imagining their possible opposition, you are more sensitive to others' feelings and more thoughtful about your choice of words. When you anticipate hostility you will be less inclined toward smugness and will come to terms with this reality: Not everyone in every situation will love you and agree with you, and that's all right! Jesus didn't do any better, so why would you expect so much?

To succeed, the speech to persuade builds on the speech to inform and progresses through the following steps.

Step 1. Begin with an introduction as in any speech, but do not give your ultimate intent when first stating the theme. For instance, a rookie salesman said, "Today, I want to get you for my customer." No one wants to be had. Instead, he could have said, "Today, I'd like to show you some products I think you'll like." Such statements as "I am here to change your mind about . . . ," or "I am going to convince you that . . ." immediately raise the listener's defenses. Your theme statement should ease the audience gently into your idea: "Let's consider for a moment . . . ," "Today we'll explore . . . ," or "We'll examine the issue of . . ." work much better.

Step 2. After you have gently and inoffensively eased into your topic, educate the audience. This is the informative part of your speech. Here, lay the foundation for the rest of the speech with facts and evidence. The audience must first understand the issue before any change can result. When supplied with proof they will better trust you and your information. This background is a necessary footing for change.

Step 3. A need or problem must be clearly pointed out to the audience if they are to take action. Meet the audience at the point of their humanity, where they live and struggle, where something is lacking in their lives. Touch the home front, relating to their basic needs as Christians and people.

One woman had a personal campaign against pornography. In neighborhoods where she spoke she purchased pornographic film and literature. Many people were simply not aware that the problem existed so close to home until viewing her display. She showed with evidence a problem existed.

Step 4. Now the members of the audience realize their needs, so don't leave them wringing their hands. Never leave the audience at the cross without the hope of salvation. It is not enough to convince them they are sinners, that people are starving, that abuse exists in their neighborhoods; they need specific and realistic remedies.

Come to the rescue. Show direction. Give your answer to the ugly picture you have just painted. Spend as much time on the problem as necessary without belaboring the issue. Spend at least the same amount of time on the answer. Relate in practical ways the solution you propose.

Step 5. Conclude by telling the audience exactly what you would like them to do. Challenge them directly. Here you can be a bit more assertive. Be sure to tell them of your intended involvement. "I'll be there, won't you join me?" They will be more likely to jump on the bandwagon if you are already on it.

In the persuasive speech the audience grows by doing. You are asking something of them this time: a commitment to read the Bible, change their lives, or simply sign up for a committee. The final echo of persuasion is: "Do something."

Most persuasion is for the long term. God is the campaign manager; we are the workers. If in one speech hundreds of lives are changed, you can be sure many went before you to plant seeds and water them. If in one speech you have fifty volunteers where only ten are needed, know you did not do this alone.

Great results from one speech are rare. Your speech may be a seed, a nutrient, a little watering of God's ideas. Still, all the little tending and weeding is necessary. The blossom is God's handiwork.

What is the measure of a good persuasive speech? How will you know you've achieved your desired results? You may never know. Not all results are measurable. A change of heart is not readily seen, nor is a deeper prayer life soon evident to the casual observer. But the eternal value of your seed planting is seen by God and felt by those affected by your words, perhaps forever.

Work Sheet

1. Draft the story of your own conversion to Christ according to the guidelines presented in this chapter. Write a five-minute version, then expand it to a forty-five-minute speech.
2. Write a persuasive speech about an issue of importance to you. Check it against the four principles of persuasion. Even if you never give this speech, you will be better ready to argue your viewpoint should the issue arise in conversation.
3. Write a how-to speech about something you could teach others: a craft, skill, or Scripture lesson.

Part **3**

Polish

9

What Do I Do With My Hands?
Discovering your natural delivery skills

"Do not be afraid of them, for I am with you to deliver you,"
declares the LORD. Then the LORD stretched out His hand and
touched my mouth.

Jeremiah 1:8, 9

We all know there are many working parts to our bodies, but did you know many of them speak besides our mouths? Face, eyes, hands, feet, elbows, shoulders all have a way of betraying us with messages. The body has a language of its own. Who we are, what we feel and believe are communicated loudly and clearly by our bodies.

Psychologists have known for years at least half of every message is sent by our bodies, and sometimes up to as

129

much as eighty percent. Most of the rest is in the tone of voice. Our actual words come in last place.[1]

What is the meaning of all this? My son demonstrated it well. One day after school I asked him, "Casey, why haven't you been bringing home any papers from school?" He immediately looked at the floor. Then forcing a big, quivering smile while still gazing down, he responded, "I lost them?" He had lost them all right, in the wastebasket at school because of bad grades.

Being his mother I wanted to believe his words; but I knew whenever there is conflict among the messages of the body, voice, and words, the truth always lies in the body. His tone of voice and body language together spoke more loudly than his words.

What we speakers communicate must be consistent with our beliefs and attitudes, or how we say it will give away our true feelings. If we are spiritually out of joint the audience will know it. All the technique in the world will not hide a self-righteous attitude or a condemning heart.

So what is a person to do with all these parts that are chattering away?

Your voice and body tell how you feel about yourself. But much insecurity and nervousness can be masked by using William James's "as if" principle mentioned in chapter 2. Walk as if you mean it, stand as if you are confident, speak out as if you are not afraid. It is yourself who will be convinced as well as the audience.

Technique is important to a good delivery. The purest Christian this side of heaven is an ineffective communicator when she appears to have soaked too long in the starch. The sincere Christian needs skills to effectively communi-

1. Albert Mehrabian, "Communication Without Words," *Psychology Today* (September 1968):53.

cate. These skills are the "how" you will add to what you say.

The Grand Entrance

In chapter 5 we discussed writing into your speech the factors for gaining audience attention. But before you begin, much is communicated. The best attention getter for the opening of your speech is you. You've heard of the grand entrance? How you move into any situation can make a difference between going unnoticed and being the center of attention.

Be dynamic. To succeed in drawing people to God, move quickly to the podium and continue the pace. Walk as if you mean it. Stand with certainty, focus confidently on your audience, and tackle that microphone as though you know you'll come out the winner. This behavior captures the audience before you speak.

With a quick glance the audience decides unconsciously whether or not you are someone worth hearing. This decision is based on the nonverbal message. How you move to the podium is a measure of your confidence and competence, and an indicator of what is to come.

At a conference, I observed two professional women. One approached the podium in a graceful trot, a peppy posture, smiling and chatting before reaching the stage steps. She moved swiftly across the stage, glowing with pleasant anticipation of the day's activities. The audience shared her anticipation. The other approached the podium at a snail's pace, with a bent posture; somber and smileless, she flatly read the day's events. She appeared ill and communicated disinterest.

To gain and maintain the audience's attention throughout your speech, you need to learn delivery skills of your body and voice. Each part has an advantage and liability all its own.

The face

The mouth is the most active part of your face even when it isn't speaking. With a flick of the lips the entire face can express a hundred different feelings. Often terror is all the audience sees, because it overtakes positive emotions. Therefore, the face must be trained to counter what is felt with what you want to communicate. You can't smile and be sour at the same time. So, if you are happy, notify your face!

Your facial expression should be consistent with the situation and the content of your speech. The smile is almost always appropriate, even in somber situations. Christians have hope, and that is something about which to smile. Sometimes, however, out of nervousness you may smile inappropriately. This is a result of not being mentally connected with your words. If you really think about what you are saying and not about yourself, your face will express the same message as your words.

The eyes

Much poetry and song has been written about eyes. They truly are globes which reflect the depths of our being. Joy and pain blink like neon from our eyes, and little can be done to cover these emotions short of closing our lids. So who's going to notice from the audience? Some will. Eyes that are alive and radiant can be seen at great distances.

There is more. The eyes do things that communicate uneasiness of various sorts. They dash across faces, never connecting with other eyes, glance nervously at clocks, and look to heaven for a cue card.[2]

2. Arch Lustberg, *Winning at Confrontation* (Washington, D.C.: U.S. Chamber of Commerce, 1984), p. 31.

I'll never forget shaking hands with President Gerald Ford when he was in office. He looked me right in the eye. No racing ahead or distracted glances, but a steady focus that communicated great presence of mind.

To master this ability of looking into faces, find a pivotal person in your audience. She is the great exhorter, someone who smiles and nods you through your speech, and even laughs at your jokes. She is obviously delighted with everything you say, and from her you gain courage to face the yawners and frowners. Always come back to this person when your ego needs recharging.

At a retreat I attended, one speaker in an over-crowded room looked only at the persons seated directly in front of her. Those of us standing along the side lost interest and drifted into whispered conversation. Everyone, not just some, in the audience needs your eyes.

The hands

The question I'm asked most often about giving a speech is, "What do I do with my hands?" Well, what do you usually do with your hands? They hang at your side until needed. You hands-and-body movements are natural outgrowths of a sincere and enthusiastic delivery. Consequently, they will generally take care of themselves. Hands demonstrate a point, make an exclamation mark, reach out to the audience, *or* betray your nervousness by picking at the wart on your left elbow.

Hands should stay off your face and resist scratching and pulling at things. Keep potential toys out of their reach. Microphone cords, jewelry, and pencils tend to become security blankets if you are not careful. Some speakers need their hands in motion to help pull words from their mouths. Others do not. Either is fine.

The feet

I was surprised when a student evangelist asked if it is all right to move around on stage. Of course it is! Feet should go with the flow of your speech. Professionals know this and use it to their advantage.

When I heard Judge Ziegler was going to speak, I couldn't resist going to hear him. No, he's not a judge but he did break the world's record for selling the most pots and pans in one year. I *knew* he had to be good, and he was. He kangarooed across the stage, down the steps, in the aisles, or was dangling his feet in the orchestra pit. This man rarely stood still. He had handouts, pots and pans, slides, and even chicken cooking on stage. We saw, heard, and smelled his speech. He didn't just stand there with his teeth hanging out; he showed us, and stimulated every taste bud in the audience.

Force your feet to come out from behind the podium on at least two occasions: the beginning and the end of your speech. This removes the podium barrier and creates a closeness with the audience. At the beginning it gives the appearance of confidence and competence. Doing the same thing at the end of your speech creates a subtle signal of its close. It also regains the audience's attention and reestablishes that relationship which may have become lost in your sea of words.

Let your feet take you across the stage in a natural way. Just make sure that if you are not walking, your feet are not talking a language of their own.

Your hands and feet will betray your nervousness if you don't tame them. When I was a kid growing up in Detroit, Soupy Sales had a children's television show on which he did a move called the Soupy Shuffle. I see a lot of feet still doing that dance during speeches. Stand or walk, but don't dance at the podium.

Hands are another big distractor. They will wander off on their own if not disciplined. Pushing up your glasses three hundred times, scratching your neck, and twisting your wedding ring are common misbehaviors.

I've seen well-educated people who weren't professional speakers do another thing — chew gum. This always fascinates me. I can't help wonder where they stick it when they are talking. The upper gum? Lower? Under the tongue? Or are they relocating it between chews? An amazing skill, but also distracting, especially if you choke on it.

Whatever you do with your body at the podium should be purposeful and facilitate the message rather than distract from it.

Vocal Skill

The voice is a versatile and powerful vehicle. It races up and down with ease, moves forward at a variety of speeds, and can stop on a dime. Its influence over words is so great as to change their meaning with a simple adjustment.

Outstanding vocal skills can so carry a speech that all other delivery skills could be done without. Once, I listened to a professional on tape. He was exciting, dynamic, inspiring, and full of energy. I imagined him to be a large man moving about in great sweeping motions as he spoke. Then I had an opportunity to see him speak. He never left the podium, and he was short, but he had such a tall voice!

Volume

Being heard is critical. If listeners must strain to hear, they will soon tire and tune out the speaker. This is serious; if no one is listening, why talk? Usually a microphone is available, but inexperienced speakers often approach it as they would a cobra about to strike. If there is a microphone, don't be afraid of it — use it.

Volume does not mean screaming. It is a pushing of the voice from the diaphragm. Erect posture is important to volume. When standing straight you have a greater capacity for air and therefore gain more force behind your vocalizations.

Timidity always is communicated by lack of volume. On stage you think you are speaking more loudly than you really are, so don't hold back.

For my fine friends with the soft, sweet voices a word of caution. Put some force and volume behind those melodic sounds or no one will pay attention. Any time a listener must strain and work to hear, she will soon give up.

Loudness must be balanced with softness. A stage whisper suddenly thrown in can immediately grab the audience, because it is different. This is not an actual whisper; while maintaining volume a hush is added to the voice.

When you are nervous about speaking your vocal cords tighten, causing the pitch of your voice to rise. I once listened to a wonderfully sincere evangelist. She was so excited that as she spoke her voice became higher and higher until it was grating. Always make an effort to speak in a deep voice. Depth is perceived as authority. The tendency of your voice is to become higher from tension, so if you shoot low your voice will come out just about normal.

Speed

The speed at which you speak affects your delivery in a number of ways. The audience can comprehend four to six times faster than you can speak, provided your articulation is clear and volume adequate.[3] However, this does not give

3. Paul E. Nelson and Judy C. Pearson, *Confidence in Public Speaking*, 2d ed. (Dubuque, Iowa: William C. Brown, 1984), p. 257.

license to go pell mell through a speech at top speed. The rate of your speech needs to be varied and broken with pauses.

A voice rate put in cruise control is boring. Slow down and speed up, but never keep the same rate throughout your speech. A slower rate is needed in two instances. First, when you are giving complicated information such as statistical data, explaining a complex relationship, or anything abstract, a slower rate facilitates greater comprehension. Second, a changed pace gives emphasis to what you say. Important points require slowing down and articulating carefully.

The rest of the time keep your rate lively. Because we are able to anticipate what is coming next if the rate is too slow, a pokey speaker soon loses the audience. Listeners, especially those at lengthy conferences, need to be pepped up, not lulled to sleep.

Expression

Vocal expression involves many factors. It is inflection, pitch — simply the upness and downness of the voice. Some refer to this as tone of voice. Whatever you call it, its influence over words is enormous. Plan to control vocal expression; otherwise, it will go off on its own, giving a message you'd prefer it didn't. The subtleties of the voice cannot be heard on paper, but let me try to explain.

"Oh," for instance, can be colored by the voice to have a variety of meanings. A short questioning response to a remark will elicit an "$_{O}$h?" When you come from the grocery store to discover a flat tire you might moan, "^{O}hh$_{hh}$." An insightful response to seeing God at work in a situation would bring a warm "O^{h}h." An abrupt, vocal resignation to bad news would be "O."

Sometimes a bad mood unrelated to the speech content

will sneak into your voice and distort the intended message. Inflection gives so many shades of meaning, be sure it is consistent with your words and purpose of your speech.

The pause

Paul Harvey is a master of the pause. At the end of his radio broadcast he always closes with "Good day," but we never know when he is going to say it. He always pauses for different lengths of time, creating a cliff-hanging effect for loyal listeners. It becomes a game with me to try to guess just when he will culminate his talk.

The silent pause is a tool. When creatively used it can have a dramatic effect or aid comprehension. It is an oasis of rest for both the speaker and listener, giving the listener's mind an opportunity to finish processing that last bit of information it has just received. When this is done the mind is more receptive to what follows. In this state of rest the mind can give much more attention to the following remarks. The pause, then, helps audience comprehension and draws attention to important parts of the speech.

Some pauses are not so silent. They pass noisily. Lips smack, crackle, and pop; or pauses "hum" and "awh" and are filled with throat clearings. Speakers are afraid of silence. For the speaker seconds drag by like hours, but only she, not the audience, has difficulty with this passage of time. In her nervous response she fills the silences with sound — not even real words, just noise. The effectiveness of the pause is then lost.

The common denominator of these four vocal skills is variety. Variety is the spice of any speech. Variety is the opposite of a monotone, the endless cross of a droning speaker. Be loud and soft, quick and slow, fluid and stopped, high and low, but not exclusively one or the other.

A pause in your words, change of rate and pace, and

other vocal dynamics catch audience attention and alert them to an upcoming change. Vocal variety, when combined with moving from the podium or a steady gaze at the audience, is the best way to underscore what you are saying or to signal the close of your speech.

Practice

Rehearse. To many well-meaning Christians this word grates against their spirituality. I wondered about it myself for quite some time. There is beauty in the unadulterated outpouring of a new Christian's heart, and I am moved by the rough-sawn testimonies of those people who have lived long lives in simple Christian faith. No doubt this authenticity is the necessary foundation of an effective delivery, and some are greatly gifted in conveying this. But they are the exceptions.

A rare jewel is made even more lovely by cutting and polishing. After the cutting and polishing, however, the ruby is still a ruby; it does not change into a pearl. The polishing touches of practice do not change who you are or who God is. Practice of delivery skills does not falsify your testimony, but helps communicate it better and reach more souls for Christ.

Many Christian speakers think preparation prevents the Holy Spirit from speaking through them. But he can speak just as well during practice as he can during the real thing. Don't limit his performance to the stage.

When we take to the podium for the first time we feel awkward. When talking to a friend there is natural inflection, appropriate volume, gesturing, and vocal expression. At the podium we lose this natural ability. But the best delivery skills are not copied or contrived in any way. They are taken from what comes naturally (which is different for each person.) Pruning, polishing, and practicing mold these qualities into the best possible vehicles for communicating God's message through us.

To rediscover your spontaneous speaking abilities first practice out loud. Allow your body and voice to do what comes naturally. Then repeat the process in front of a full-length mirror while recording your voice. Video taping is even better.

While watching yourself, evaluate your body message from the viewpoint of the audience. Where are your hands? Scratching your head, pulling your ear, or clinging to each other for emotional support? Are they flying around naturally and moving with the content of the message? Mentally register what adds to and detracts from the message and edit appropriately. Eliminate annoying mannerisms. Limit and exaggerate appropriate ones, but remember, too much repetition becomes monotonous.

From the audience everything on stage appears minimized. Timid motion will be missed. If your hands are making a point, the motion must be bigger than normal. This feels awkward at first, but developing this skill will enhance your delivery effectiveness.

What is your face doing? Are you looking in the mirror more than at your papers? Are you smiling appropriately and often? Are you scanning the audience with your eyes? Does your facial expression reflect the content of the message?

Are your feet behaving, or doing the Soupy Shuffle? Do you shift your weight from side to side? Or habitually stick your hand on your hip? Is your posture the best it can be without rigor mortis setting in?

The extent of your sincerity is reflected in your face. Is it expressive, smiling, or twitching? Is it warm and open, or closed with tension?

Now listen to your tape recording. Is this someone you would listen to for an hour? Is your articulation clear? Does your volume drop at the ends of sentences? Are expression and variety abundant in your voice? Is there obvious energy and enthusiasm? Is "umm" or "so" used too often? Do you smack your lips, crack your knuckles, or habitually sigh?

The goal of practice and self-evaluation is to refine individual qualities. Borrowing the gestures of a favorite evangelist will not lead to a successful delivery. Be genuine, but with quality control.

Notes on Notes

Preparing notes for delivery gives your speech a polished result. Use five-by seven-inch cards or white typing paper. Put notes on only one side. As you change sheets slide the top one to one side rather than turning it. This way notes are not distracting and rattles are not picked up by the microphone. Be sure to end each page with a natural stopping point so there is not an inappropriate pause while you refocus on the next point on the following page.

I like to write my notes rather than type them. In the process of writing, the order of the speech is more firmly planted in my mind. Using a modified version of the traditional outline, I write out the lead-in statement for each section. Under each statement I list in order of presentation the key words of subpoints, anecdotes, and examples to be used. If there is critical phrasing necessary for humor or setting a serious tone, I write these out word-for-word and indicate the timing. For instance, if I am switching topics I might write a big *pause* at the end of the previous subpoints.

Use color. I've seen the notes of professionals, and often they will highlight in yellow a critical statement or underline something important. Color coding helps draw your attention to a special note when scanning ahead.

I write notes about delivery in green. *Pause, smile,* or *look at audience* are found along the margins of my notes. Statements needing extra vocal force are underlined in red. These delivery cues help prevent timing mistakes and gain the effect I want.

Use of the outline and key-word method will trigger a concept or anecdote. The content is the same each time the speech is given, but choice of words, phrasing, and delivery will vary, adding the element of spontaneity and sincerity.

Do not write out your speech word-for-word. If you do, you will be tempted to read it word-for-word. Reading a speech is deadly. You cannot be flexible enough to adapt to the audience, and the speech sounds stilted and dull, lacking the life of your personality. It also limits eye contact and delivery skills, because you are chained to the manuscript. If you lose a page, or pages somehow become out of order, you will be stuck "winging it" and being poorly prepared for the job.

Memorizing a speech is to be equally discouraged. Remember, speech anxiety causes the brain to quit working. In that moment of fear you will find yourself both speechless and noteless. Even those times when you don't forget, you are inflexible, stuck in a predetermined word rut.

Memorizing *small parts* of your speech is fine. This facilitates a smooth flow. The introduction is the best part to memorize, because it is here that the tendency to lose your eyes in your notes is the greatest. Other short sections or phrases can be memorized when exact wording is important to your point. The conclusion is also best if memorized so you can give the audience one-hundred percent of your attention.

There is no heavenly mold marked *Christian Speaker* into

which God pours us. Molds are for cutting cookies, not people. A dynamic delivery involves your individuality being polished, not the cloning of mechanics and performance. Speakers should not be homogenized, or just as in the milk, the cream will no longer rise to the top. God is not limited to one mode of expression. He spoke through Balaam's donkey, through fishermen, children, and murderers. He can speak through you.

Work Sheet

1. Practice one of your speeches in front of a mirror. Notice what habits you may have that will distract the audience. Ask someone to tell you when he notices these habits in your casual conversation. This will assist you in bringing your voice and body under conscious control.
2. Study standup comedians. What do they do through voice and body language to solicite audience response?
3. In a mall or restaurant observe people in casual conversation. How do they use their bodies? What do they do nonverbally to help communicate their messages?

10

The Magnetic Speaker
Developing Your Image

Create in me a clean heart, O God, And renew a steadfast spirit within me. Do not cast me away from Thy presence, And do not take Thy Holy Spirit from me. Restore to me the joy of Thy salvation, And sustain me with a willing spirit. Then I will teach transgressors Thy ways, And sinners will be converted to Thee.
Psalm 51:10–13

So here you are at center stage. Your hands and feet are nicely trained, but there is more, so much more. The Christian speaker is not putting on an act, but living out a truth. A magnetic speaker is the offspring of a marriage between outward mechanics and inner living.

I Haven't Got a Thing to Wear

When I was at a Christian retreat I decided not to listen to a particular speaker. But when the other workshops filled, she was my only option. Unconsciously, I had ruled her out,

145

not on the basis of credentials or topic, but on the way she looked. When she was introduced I knew she couldn't know anything. Her hair was out of style and so was her dress. She wore a brown, topstitched jumper, too youthful for her advanced years, and a bandanna around her neck. All in all, I knew she was planning to ride off on her horse immediately after speaking.

By the time she had completed her presentation I was totally humbled. She moved me to tears, and all I could do was hug her in appreciation before I left. I almost missed an excellent talk because of my preconceived notions of what a good speaker *should* look like.

In the last chapter we discussed the messages sent by the voice and body. What we wear is a message system as well. John T. Molloy has done extensive research on clothing. He says hairdos, nail polish, makeup, color combinations, handbags, and even the ink pens we use send messages.[1] Although Molloy is addressing professionals in the business world, his research is a legitimate consideration for Christian women, also, for we may sometimes address professionals who will judge us by these standards. Furthermore, much of what he says applies to any occupation and is worth studying.

We speakers need to remember that even the Christian audience will judge our worth by our appearance. Studies prove it. We know we can speak truth just as easily in purple hair and a minskirt as in a pinstriped suit. If the audience cannot get beyond what they see, however, they will not hear. Although who we are in Christ is more important than what we wear, it is also true that what we wear will be the deciding factor in who the audience *thinks* we are.

1. John T. Molloy, *The Woman's Dress for Success Book* (New York: Warner Books, 1977), p. 62.

The obsession with fashion in this country has bothered me for a long time, but fashion in clothing has been with us since Bible days. The ministry of Dorcas was to fashion clothes for friends and strangers, many of whom wandered the beaches of Joppa looking for rags to wear. Their lack of clothes seriously affected their lives. Later, her ministry spread far beyond her small community.

Lydia, the seller of purple, reminds us clothes of that color were a status symbol in Bible times.[2] The ideal woman of Proverbs 31 dressed in fine linen and purple and dressed her household in scarlet, the best material in her day.

Society's current dictates of acceptable dress is the standard by which we are first measured. Then, if we pass inspection, what we have to say might be received. Unfortunately, as loving and accepting as we Christians like to think we are, we are subject to our own critical attitudes as much as anyone. We do not see the heart of a woman, because we cannot see past her crooked hemline. God's word predicts this: "Man looks at the *outward* appearance, but the LORD looks at the heart" (1 Sam. 16:7).

For too long the typical Christian has been viewed as a bag lady with a cross around her neck. This stereotypical image lives on. One professional told me she was at a conference for Christian speakers. That week the hotel had a western theme, so she dressed accordingly in cowboy boots, hat and skirt. When she introduced herself to the manager he was shocked. "I didn't expect you to look like that!" he blurted out when he saw her getup. "I expected a little old lady with a bun, long dress, and Bible tucked under her arm!"

So, how do we dress to speak?

2. Edith Deen, *All the Women of the Bible* (New York: Harper and Row, 1955), p. 219.

Dressing

Each audience needs a speaker with whom they can identify, someone who is dressed in a way that is not drastically
different from their own. This means not wearing a designer
gown to speak to the underprivileged, or blue jeans to speak
to professional women. Your clothing must be currently in
style, but not high fashion; authoritative without being
overbearing.

Quality and simplicity are the key words according to
wardrobe consultant, Emily Lite. These guidelines are consistent with research and with biblical principles. The ideal
woman in Proverbs 31 dressed in the best fabric and the
color of royalty. She serves as an example of quality. Paul
also wrote about women's clothing in terms such as *modest,
discreet* and *not extreme* (1 Tim. 2:9). In a time of rainbow-
colored hair and six-inch baubles hanging from female ear
lobes, simplicity could surely use a comeback!

A well-made suit or dress, plain or with a small design
in a subdued color, is ideal for most speaking situations. If
you have one or two nice outfits, you can wear them to
almost all your speaking engagements.

Remove anything that might be offensive or distracting
about your appearance. A woman who has ministered to
me many times looks like a prostitute. It hurts me to hear
her criticized, yet I realize her excess makeup, jewelry, and
clothes are barriers to her effectively reaching many. Training
director and seminar leader for Image Products, Inc., cos-
metologist Diane Peyton, told me, "A lot is never good."[3]

As speakers, we are to draw attention to God, not ourselves. A story Billy Graham tells illustrates this perfectly:

> I remember when I started preaching. I was in a little
> church in Florida where forty or fifty people were present.

3. Diane Peyton (Telephone interview).

My father had given me a wristwatch when I graduated
from high school; it had a gold band, and I remember I
looked down, and it shone in the light. I saw a couple of
people looking at it. The Lord said to me, "Take that off.
It's distracting."

I said, "Lord, I can surely wear a wristwatch that my
daddy gave me." But it was sensitivity that God was teaching me — to be sensitive to the little things. I took it off and
put it in my pocket. I never wore it in the pulpit again.[4]

Although Molloy's studies prove particular styles, accessories, and colors produce better results, no scientific survey can factor in the Spirit of God living within the speaker.
John the Baptist wasn't exactly a fashion plate in his animal
skins. I'm sure we would all be disappointed if Nobel Peace
laureate Mother Teresa donned a New York coiffure, nylons,
and pumps to meet the press. The world would be disgusted
with her commercialization. It is she who said, "To know
oneself and not be untrue is the essence of living."[5] She is
true to herself and her God.

These are the exceptions. God does call people to speak
and minister in spite of their wardrobes. But quality and
simplicity should nevertheless be your guidelines, unless
you have a special ministry; a black leather jacket *can* touch
where a pinstriped suit could never reach. Be sensitive to
God's leading and sensitive to your audience. You will then
know where you are to go and what you are to wear.

Love: The Image of God

We project an image which is composed of two parts.
The one is physical. Cosmetically, we can do much these

4. Billy Graham, "Time — You Will Never Live This Minute Again," *Decision*
(January 1985):3.
5. Curtis Bill Pepper, "I'm a Little Pencil in God's Hand," *McCall's* (March
1980):82.

days to look good. How we dress and adorn ourselves has an impact on the audience. This part of our image is literally put on. The other part of our image overrides all the rest. It can never be put on, but only brought out. It is the image of God residing within us.

When I was at a women's witnessing conference, someone commented, "God must love beautiful women. Did you notice how gorgeous all the speakers are?" They truly were, and I got to thinking about that. What made these women so beautiful? It wasn't the world's value of beauty. It was a quality that flowed from within. These women loved God, and *that* made them beautiful. God's glowers, like beautiful flowers in a desert, attract the lost. People want to be with those who have seen him.

We are to love, each of us. Love is a drawing force that pulls even the most resistant person closer to God.

> Though I'm eloquent, humorous, profound, knowledgeable, and dynamic; whether I can hold an audience in my grip and mesmerize individuals with my gifts and personality, without love it is empty and just noise.[6]

This paraphrase of 1 Corinthians 13:1 especially applies to Christian speakers.

The Bible says without love we are as a noisy gong or a clanging cymbal (1 Cor. 13:1). And how about you? How do you sound? Are you brassy and abrasive, filled with negativism? Are you sounding a gong or beating a cymbal, making earthly music about heavenly issues? Love is the melodic symphony that tempers our words with heavenly harps.

God's gifts to us are to be regulated by love. We are to love first, *then* go and tell the world. If we cannot love our

6. Myrl Glochner (Bible study conducted in Wheaton, Ill., 10 July 1985).

students and feed them with tenderness, then we'll give them indigestion with the message.

Love cannot be manufactured for the moment. The veneer of insincerity wears out quickly. Human love can only flow from the deep well of God's love. As Christians, we have no right to use our skills and talents if they are not outgrowths of love. The empty rhetoric of someone who lives a great distance from God is quickly recognized. A loveless person drives spiritually and emotionally healthy people in the opposite direction.

We are obligated when indwelt by God, who is love, to show this love to others. Loving our audience is the most important element we can bring to public speaking. This spiritual posture supersedes bad attitudes, nerves, and even our own incompetence. Sincere love is the most important delivery skill, a powerful magnet that draws heavy metal hearts close to him.

Love will show in your words. Not only relating what God has done for you, but your vocabulary will reflect the tone of your heart. Anger, bitterness, and unforgiveness creep into the vocabulary and kill the foliage of love trying so hard to blossom there. I'm guilty, and so are you.

Love is that special ring in earthbound angelic voices. Love is the special power that draws others to Christ. Love is God, and God is in the magnetic speaker.

The Cheerleader

For some reason, many Christians mistakenly think any display of emotion is unspiritual. At a Christian conference I was gaily hopping down three flights of steps at 6:30 A.M. in anticipation of another great day. I flew past a well-known Christian writer/editor dragging himself up the stairs.

"Good morning!" I exclaimed.

"Slow down," was his condemning response.

The act of hiding joy is a crime. The world observes Christians who, "look like they've been weaned on a dill pickle."

"Who needs *that*?" they think, and rightly so.

You've seen the type: Pious Polly Perfect, dripping with reserve and looking like someone had stuck a steel rod up her back. Nothing against good posture, it's important, but we need to communicate earthliness. I saw Polly in a panel, once. Before it was her turn to speak, I *knew* I didn't like her. She sat perched on the edge of her chair, dressed drably, with her lips pursed so tightly together they had to be numb. She may be a very nice person who loves the Lord and lives a holy life, but if she *is*, no one knows it.

Where is the joy?

People danced, sang, and rejoiced their way through the Bible. Solomon rejoiced in his bride, in joy David praised God unceasingly, and the heavens rejoice when one sinner repents. Be positive about your faith. The Bible exclaims the joy of salvation. Many experience this when their faith is new, only to lose it along the way. My good friend Don Mainprize put it this way in *Enjoy The Christian Life*: "To hear them speak, one might conclude that their God passed away shortly after their salvation."[7]

Joy does not consist of the giddy good times the world calls happiness. Even in our losses, Paul said, we must count it all joy. Joy is a hope that thrives in all circumstances.

Where did we get the warped idea Christianity is dull and unemotional? We are to rejoice in our salvation. We are commanded to love. We are to be either hot or cold, but not lukewarm. The Bible is filled with intensity and passion. Floods, miracles, plagues, healing, love, tears were not sent by a passive God.

7. Don Mainprize, *Enjoy the Christian Life* (Wheaton, Ill.: Tyndale, 1966), p. 108.

We Christians need to be cheerleaders, energetically encouraging everyone to excellence in Christ. Everyone needs an encourager standing on the sidelines saying, "You can do it! Keep going! Never give up!" Motivational speakers know this. They travel cross country for corporations and other organizations and make big bucks pumping employees full of self-esteem. Direct sales companies know this as well. They hoot, holler, and cheer their distributors into success.

No doubt this kind of psychological support pushes many an athlete that extra painful mile, a little bit faster, driving her beyond the limits she thought she had.

Enthusiasm is individually expressed. We are not all foot stompin', hand clappin', holy ya-hooers. There are times when we must be still. But any degree of enthusiasm adds new energy to our gait, a sparkle to our eye, and dynamically invades our choice of words.

Has someone asked you to speak? Then you should be excited — excited about the opportunity to share, build, give, in the name of Christ. Isn't he the most important person to you? God's Word drives this point home: "And I will punish the men who are stagnant in spirit" (Zeph. 1:12).

Just as a moment of sun will cheer our hearts on an otherwise gray winter day, we must be the bright spots in other's winters, so lively and vivid they can't help but enjoy our spirit even if they disagree with our words.

Enthusiasm and joy are the evident fruits of our relationship with Christ. Enthusiasm actually means to be inspired by God. We must not limit his presence in us by our own inhibitions. If you are speaking for him and you're not excited, something is wrong.

We need to be the visible evidence of his presence. We should go off like Christian sparklers, exploding in the skies as if every day were the Fourth of July, a celebration of life eternal, forever with him.

The Fragrance of Christ

Her hair was angelic gold, her white dress flowed softly over her fragile frame, and she glowed. Joy rang in her voice, and peace penetrated the tiny country church. Her speaking was surely inspired, for no one could live out what she had and not know God.

Goldie Bristol is not a household name, but you may have read her story. In 1978, she and her husband traveled across the country to a prison. There they embraced the man convicted of the rape and murder of their twenty-one-year-old daughter.

Her faith was surely tried and tested. She of all people had reason to be bitter. Yet, she exchanged the human tendency to withdraw when hurt for a speaking ministry. She preaches forgiveness across the country, and many broken relationships have been restored because of her.

This is the Scripture text Goldie Bristol gave me that day. It applies to all of us, especially speakers. "But thanks be to God who always leads us in His triumph in Christ, and manifests through us the sweet aroma of the knowledge of Him in every place" (2 Cor. 2:14).

Do you leave a lingering fragrance of Christ wherever you go?

First, sweep the inner stage clean. Pride, selfishness, unconfessed sin, anything that could short circuit the Holy Spirit's work through us must go. Vonette Bright told a delightful story about her husband and son that illustrates this point. Once, when they were playing with an electric train, it suddenly stopped. Her husband took apart the train and track in an attempt to locate the problem. An hour later he noticed a tiny piece of metal on the track. When he removed it the train began to run.[8]

We stop the even greater power of the Holy Spirit in the same way. Sin will tinge the atmosphere around us. A tiny fleck of smugness or self-satisfaction can stop him cold in his tracks. Our lives need to be right with God to keep on a-chuggin'.

Second, submit your words and efforts to God for his use. We need to get out of his way. I once watched a speaker giving a narrative on an important point. Caught in her ego she dramatically tossed the script page by page while a tinseled halo slipped down the side of her head. The point was lost in the performance. The atmosphere was not sweet with Christ but tainted with her self.

Before beginning a workshop, author and teacher Evelyn Christenson prayed, "Lord, we don't want a speaker. Remove the speaker right now. We only want to see you." We can pray no less. In spite of the effort we put into learning technique, our delivery must be clean of self and full of him. The message is his. We are only the tools. How self-right-eous is a hammer or a saw? We should be as inconspicuous and clean as the window through which the sun beams, especially in the temple that houses God.

Third, we must live God's script for our lives — the Bible. To do this we must know it, then act on it. A Christian life cannot be contrived. Wise Christians immediately sense from where our leading comes.

Professional speaker Ty Boyd tells a story that beautifully demonstrates the power of God's indwelling image. It supersedes talent, technique, and words.

> Charles Lawton, a great English actor, was touring Ameri-ca doing one-night performances. Part of his program was

8. Vonette Bright (Speech delivered in Wheaton, Ill., 9 July 1985).

to read from the Bible. Though he had learned the lines a long time ago, he still held the Bible up as a prop.

One evening in a theater he held that Bible up, and looking up from his lines, saw in the back of the room an old gentleman standing flagging him. Though it wasn't part of the program, Lawton stopped. He looked at the old gentleman and said, "Yes, may I help you?" the old man said, "I, too, would like to read from the Bible."

Charles Lawton invited him up. The old man probably had never been on the stage before, certainly not with the likes of that great, English actor. Charles Lawton offered him the Bible, and he began cautiously to read. He selected his favorite passages and it wasn't long before he was lost in the Book reading to the people.

After the program was over Charles Lawton had gone backstage and a young reporter who was sitting out front ran backstage and started talking to Lawton. He said, "Mr. Lawton, had there been judges here tonight and had they judged you and the old man as you read from the Bible, who would have won the contest?" Charles Lawton is reported to have said, after thinking for just a moment,

"Had there been judges tonight, the old man would have won the contest."

The young reporter said, "Pray tell, how?" and Charles Lawton replied,

"Simple. You see, I knew the material, but he knew the author."[9]

Work Sheet

1. Examine yourself spiritually. Ask God to show you what he would have you change about yourself. A good resource for this activity is "*Lord, Change Me!*" by Evelyn Christenson.

9. Ty Boyd, "Right Place, Right Time" (Speech delivered in Washington, D.C., August 1982).

2. Study the model of the ideal woman in Proverbs 31. Work on those areas of your life where you fall short. Jill Briscoe's book *Queen of Hearts: The Role of Today's Woman Based on Proverbs* 31, covers this in depth.

3. Choose one or two outfits for speaking, including accessories. Do they add to your self-confidence? Do they interfere with or distract from your message? Will they cause others to have the wrong opinion of you? Remember, your clothes must help facilitate your verbal message.

Part 4

Prime

11

Cherry Pitfalls and Molasses Swamp
Problems and Considerations of Public Speakers

Help these women who have shared my struggle in the cause of the gospel.

Philippians 4:3

When my children were younger they loved to play the popular board game Candy Land.®[1] It contains a brightly colored path leading to a sugar-coated house with chocolate steps and a peppermint-stick fence. If the lure of home is great, the sweet temptations along the way are greater. Treats of every kind promise pleasure, but difficulty also lurks in cherry pitfalls, molasses swamp, and lollypop woods.

---

1. Candy Land® is a registered trademark of Milton Bradley Company.

The public-speaking trail is also brightly marked. Home is heaven, and we must keep our eyes on that mark to avoid slipping into those temptations off the path. God holds the map. He knows the way he would have us go, but often we look aside at the immediate rewards and slip into a cherry pitfall.

Pitfall 1. *Motivation*

Usually we begin reaching out to others with a pure heart, but something happens. Power, pride, and popularity lurk in lollypop woods and beckon us to go their way, to follow their wisdom.

Why are you here at this point in this book? Who wants you on that platform? Did a cloud go before you? Was manna strewn along the path? You are reading this page for a reason; is it for you or for God?

I struggled with this question several years ago. As I listened to a speaker I felt an inner nudging; something inside me whispered, "What are you afraid of? You can do it!"

"No, I can't." I fought back. "I can't handle it and I don't want to." But my protests would not still the thought. It followed me for months. Was it the Lord urging me to share my testimony, or the voice of my own faltering ego wanting recognition? I thought about my life and all my mistakes from which others could learn. How gracious the Lord had been in dealing with me, how much I had learned. But so much I didn't yet understand. There seemed no real reason for my reluctance except my slipping self-esteem. I had allowed my worth to be measured by work outside the home. After many years as a housewife and mother my confidence had eroded. I decided to take the easy way out. "Lord," I prayed, "if you want me to speak, someone will have to ask me, because I'm surely not going to volunteer."

You guessed it. Three months later I received the call.

"Nancy, would you consider speaking for one of our luncheons sometime?" What could I say?

Examine your motives. Ask yourself why you want to speak. Do you desire to serve or long for the limelight? Do you really want to help others or simply strut your spiritual stuff?

Before speaking to any group, your motives must be cleansed. Be assured your motives will be tested by Heaven and earth. Prayerfully seek God's will; don't just run away with your impulse. The glory must go to God.

Pitfall 2. Criticism

The British-born actress and author Joan Winmill Brown is no stranger to criticism. When she first came to this country as a fairly new Christian, she toured with her Christian film *Souls in Conflict*. At Carnegie Hall she stood before the crowd and explained what the Lord had done in her life. After the showing of the film, scores came forward to accept Christ. Others came to criticize.

> a little old lady came up to me, shaking her fist in my face!
> "Go back to England where you belong!" she said. "You've
> only come over here for the money — just like the English!"
> . . . another lady was also waiting to pounce on me. "Don't
> cross your legs when you are on the platform. Looks
> disgusting!"[2]

Criticism is not easy to accept, even when solicited. At the end of my first semester as a college instructor I asked my students to write an evaluation of me. They did, and some surely weren't kind! I found myself pulling out papers and comparing handwriting, trying to figure out who made the nasty remarks. Over the semesters I have learned three

2. Joan W. Brown, *No Longer Alone* (Old Tappan, N.J.:Revell, 1975), p. 81.

things from this exercise: (1) Some criticism is correct; (2) Don't ask for criticism until you are ready to take it; (3) Some ground is too hard to plow.

Public people make perfect targets. They are not hiding in homes safe from risk. They are exposing their innermost selves to scrutiny.

Criticism from unbelievers is somehow easier to accept than that from fellow Christians. I have two special critics in my life, both Christians, both men. I have no doubt their hearts' desire is to see every last sinner come to Christ. After hearing my testimony, one commented, "Not bad for a girl." Other cutting remarks are reminders of the inability of those two to accept me as a vehicle of God's work.

Norman Vincent Peale has offered this advice on criticism:

> And you will be criticized if there is any force whatsoever to your personality. There is just one way to avoid criticism: never do anything, never amount to anything. Get your head above the crowd and the jealous will notice and attack you. Therefore, welcome criticism as a sign that your life has vitality. . . . Never answer back, never explain, keep your spirit right.[3]

Criticism tends to deflate our confidence and enthusiasm. Don't let others rob you of a God-given dream. Persevere under fire and remember, "Therefore, do not throw away your confidence, which has a great reward" (Heb. 10:35).

Pitfall 3. Ego

Becoming a speaker for God is not becoming a celebrity, but a servant. How big would your ego be while washing

3. Norman Vincent Peale, *You Can Have God's Help with Daily Problems* (New York, 1980), p. 99.

twelve pairs of dusty feet? The spotlight in your eyes must not blind you to your role in the body of Christ.

The hard work is done; Christ died on the cross. Many others throughout the centuries sacrificed lives, families, and countries so the good news would survive and reach this generation. What is an ego that it cannot be crucified on the cross of public opinion?

If your ego is out of joint, it will be difficult for you to balance atop your pedestal. If some criticism is fired your way, you are sure to topple. Too much confidence is a dangerous thing. Your mouth then becomes unhinged from God and becomes the revolving door of your ego. If it is too big, ego will seep into your words and out your seams where the audience will see it.

One year when the award was given for the best Gospel music act, the recipient immediately responded, "First of all, it's not an act". Neither is public speaking. It is a life shared out of love for Christ — a service, not a show. If you see yourself as privileged, blessed, chosen, or gifted, look again. You are simply an instrument through which God can speak, the earthbound megaphone of heavenly news. It is the sincere servant heart that heaven applauds.

In a sixteenth-century letter Brother Lawrence, a Carmelite lay brother, wrote that God "isn't so much impressed with the dimensions of our work as with the love in which it is done."[4] He was a dishwasher.

We are not to be self-crowned queens of the public arena, but handmaidens of the King. As we diminish our ego into servanthood the quality of what we do for the Lord will improve. Meekness is not synonymous with mediocrity. In

4. Brother Lawrence, *The Practice of the Presence of God* (Springdale, Pa.: Whitaker House, 1985), p. 21.

a humbled state we are empowered to do great things, boldly.

Pitfall 4. *Praise*

We fuss and squirm when we are unjustly criticized, but rarely do we argue when given unearned applause. Praise is another by-product of the public life and one that needs to be handled humbly.

Pleasing the crowd is something we know better as peer pressure. We usually reserve that term for teen-agers who give in to the wild ways of their friends. But Christian adults give in, too. When I first began college teaching it was easy for me to say things I knew would titillate a group of young students. My words got laughs, my teaching techniques praise, I felt "with it," but I did not glorify God.

God's people are not crowd pleasers. We do not run with popular thought. Jesus came to save the world, not to conform to it. Loving your audience and building rapport is appeal without compromise.

If there is any group of people I have admired more than another it is Christian authors. To me, having an author sign his book is like capturing his soul. Most enjoy autographing their books for me, some much more than others, but one author did not enjoy it at all. I sensed his reluctance immediately. Later, in a speech, he expressed his concern that Christians chase after men and not God. He truly exemplified a humble servant who wrote not for money or fame, but to minister to others. His attitude is the excellence of spirit for which we must strive. After all, we can do nothing outside of Christ.

Praise can be overwhelming to the humble and head swelling to the prideful. When we do receive praise we should pass it on. If we are truly humble this will not be difficult to do. Corrie ten Boom once gave this advice about praise:

"Take all the praise of the people like a bunch of flowers and offer them as a bouquet to the Lord."[5] God inhabits praises — not those given to us, but those given to him. The only worthwhile praise we will ever hear is, "Well done, good and faithful servant" (Matt. 25:21, NIV).

Pitfall 5. Remuneration

Are we to be paid for speaking God's word and teaching his people? If so, how much? If not, who finances our speaking engagements?

Paul explained in the ninth chapter of 1 Corinthians it is right to expect to gain a living from spreading the gospel and be financially supported by those to whom we speak. Paul, however, chose not to exercise this right at all times.

I've talked with women at all points on the spectrum of opinion. Coupling their experiences with what Scripture says seems to indicate remuneration is not the issue so much as the speaker's attitude and expectations.

At one end of the financial scale is Lois. She operates her ministry entirely on faith, never asking for money nor letting her needs be made known to anyone but God. When I talked with her, someone she'd never met had just sent her the exact amount needed for her plane ticket to Israel. Another time, when she was badly in need of shoes, a woman took her shoes off and handed them to her. They both wore size ten. She also related a week she lived on popcorn and Jell-o, a time I'm sure she wished someone had been moved to be generous. Her faith was impressive.

At the other extreme is one of the top-paid Christian speakers, who receives around five thousand dollars a seminar. She found the more money she charged the more her

5. Pat Assimakopoulos, "Joan Winmill Brown: Writing in Different Genre," *The Christian Writer* (February 1985):15.

services were requested, and has doubled her rates every year.

One international speaker's experience was quite interesting. In some situations, after much personal expense and inconvenience, he might receive a small honorarium barely covering his costs. Then, in less sacrificial situations, he received large sums. He reflected that after twenty years of speaking the donations and honorariums balanced out to what he would have expected if seeking a salary.

One woman was not this satisfied with her public-speaking experience. After twenty-one years of service to a Christian organization she felt unappreciated and left the group. Often she was paid nothing for her efforts. Speakers from outside the organization were paid handsomely — an inconsistency she could not accept.

It is nice to be appreciated, especially when it takes the form of money. Speakers are paid in three ways. Those with an agent have a set fee of which the agent takes a percentage. Others have a set fee without an agent. And still others accept donations or an honorarium from the host organization. An honorarium is an unfixed amount and will vary greatly with each situation.

Paul Harvey is paid $25,000 to speak, Joyce Brothers $12,000 and Art Linkletter $10,000. Most Christian speakers never see this kind of money. I find this discrepancy interesting, since we have the most valuable information this side of heaven. When we use man's financial yardstick to measure our worth, we may find ourselves coming up wanting. Man may not give according to God's view of our value. Keep a healthy perspective, and know that you will usually be underpaid.

One speaker commented to me, "You're not going to get rich speaking for *them*." Getting rich is not the purpose. It may happen, but it is not a goal. I received thirty dollars for speaking forty-five minutes. That's more than I am paid for teaching. How much is not the issue.

When our focus is on our gain we need to get on our knees. Our focus must be on the unseen, what others will gain eternally from our giving. If a group cannot give support, we should not withhold our teaching, but gladly share our wisdom with them. As Paul wrote to the Galatians, we should not lose heart, for we will reap our eternal rewards in due time (see Gal. 6:8, 9).

If there is a need, fill it. What you do about your income is between you and God. Not everyone is called to a faith ministry nor to be a highly paid speaker. Explore your feelings honestly, explore the Bible, and speak to God. Then go about your mission secure in God's direction for you.

Pitfall 6. Help seekers

Every sixteen weeks, the length of a semester, new adults come under my instruction. The players change, but the script remains the same. They appear at my office door under the presumption of needing help with an assignment, than sigh and say, "Man, it's going to be a tough semester, because. . . ." Others spill out their bitterness and brokenness in speeches. Confessions of addiction, promiscuity, cancer, or abuse flood from their lips with great abandon. That students would so reveal themselves to an audience underscores their great need to be heard. I am certain there are unknown multitudes outside my classroom silently suffering their way through life.

As Christians who have stumbled down the path just ahead of those who hurt, we are obligated to help. Each of us is needy at some time. When any of us with the love of Christ in our hearts enters a situation, the emotionally and spiritually impoverished are drawn to his presence in us.

I've seen it happen many times. Women line up just to

have a few words with a speaker. Tearful help-seekers will catch her at the stage steps, join her for lunch, or corner her in the ladies room. One by one they share their pain. Often women go to hear a particular speaker because needs exist in their lives. The topic may appear to be a potential answer. So they come with cautious hope.

Even more than to find answers, help-seekers need to tell someone how bad it is. A sympathetic listener eases the load and may offer encouragement. If you have never been in their position, don't try to tell them you know how they feel. You don't. It is all right not to have all the answers. But it is important to direct them to the best source, God's Word, and pray with them.

Often someone's problems are so complex you feel overwhelmed by them yourself and don't know where to begin. You may not be able to help all those God brings across your path. If not, recommend professional therapy. Often, women who carry a great load alone feel inadequate because they cannot cope. By pointing out the enormity of their problem and the need for professional help you can perhaps relieve them of some of their guilt.

Being a loving sympathizer frequently offers the best antidote to a broken heart. Accommodate the burdened. Give them your time, your heart, then give them to God.

Pitfall 7. Family

When I was headlong into writing this book, staring down the barrel of a deadline, I overheard some yelling from another part of the house.

"Dad, I need my pink pleated skirt ironed," my daughter demanded in desperation.

"I don't do pleats," was my husband's response.

My husband wanted me to write this book, and he was

willing to do what was necessary to bring that about. His dishpan hands are a living testimonial.

Before you judge me too harshly, let it be known I change flat tires, fix plumbing, and stoke the woodstove regularly during our subzero winters.

As a family, we have not suffered from my extra commitments; only the house has. Plants die, wallpaper falls, and things grow on the food in my refrigerator. It is all a matter of priorities. I've never missed a soccer game, baseball game, parade, concert, play, or scout ceremony in which our kids were involved. I work hard to keep this balance of what is important. Caring for people outranks caring for things.

God didn't intend for us to toss aside our families for a greater "calling." There is a time to say no.

When I had the opportunity to hit the speaking circuit, I said no. We had undergone some enormous strains as a family. The children needed the stability of a regular schedule and dependable mom. I needed peace, rest, and a time to heal. We know that Jesus took time away from the crowds to rest, yet we women expect so much more of ourselves than God does. At the time it seemed I was throwing away an opportunity to minister; but by making this choice I was not turning my back on reaching out to others. Instead, I chose something I could do at home around my family's schedule — write.

If you are married, before you are pulled down the public path by the lure of elevated self-esteem, be sure that your marriage relationship will tolerate the strain. Both dimensions of a woman's life must be taken into consideration; if your private life withers, so will your public life.

Every family differs. Even though sharing God's love through speaking often is a good thing to do, it does not mean it is the best thing to do. Knowing God's priorities for your life will balance the tendency to overdo a good thing.

Many women are called into demanding ministries outside their homes. Such women, without exception, have told me, "I couldn't do it without my husband's support. He is one-hundred ten percent behind me."

A single speaking engagement will not throw your house-hold into total turmoil, but a speaking ministry could upset the status quo. Each family must find what works best for them. The time spent writing, traveling, and speaking will be time taken away from something else. What are you willing to sacrifice?

Work Sheet

1. Pray about each of the seven public-speaking pitfalls. Make decisions and deal with each area now before you are confronted with it. Ask yourself how you intend to cope with these issues. Ask for your family's input and support.
2. Ask God to show you any of your wrong motives for speaking, and seriously reexamine whether the public arena is the place for you.
3. Step into the public arena and give one speech to test your "calling."

12

Words from the Wise
Advice from the Experts

Give me now wisdom and knowledge.

2 Chronicles 1:10

I am fortunate to have had opportunities to hear many fine Christian women speak. Much of what I have learned by observing them has influenced this book. I asked several outstanding speakers what advice they would give to beginners. Most are willing to take time from their busy schedules to give you a few pointers. It is with heartfelt appreciation that I pass on their wisdom.

Marjorie Holmes, author of several books, including *I've Got to Talk to Somebody, God, Two From Galilee,* and her newest novel *The Young Man From Nazareth.*

1. Prepare. Rehearse. Sketch out a rough draft of your talk and practice it over and over wherever you are —

173

washing dishes, in the bathtub, or in front of a mirror, no matter, until you become so familiar with it you could almost throw your notes away.

2. *Never* read your speech (the quickest way to put people to sleep!) And never learn it by heart. It should sound natural, spontaneous, however, well-organized. This is what preparation and rehearsal will accomplish for you.

3. Be natural, be friendly, and wherever appropriate, be funny. No matter how serious the subject, people also like to be amused.

4. Don't be afraid because the audience is large. A thousand people, or a hundred, are simply that many *individuals*. Years ago I taught myself that I am actually talking to just one person. *Each one* there.

5. There is an old adage for speakers: "Be there, be brief, be gone." While I wouldn't go that far, I agree with the late Dale Carnegie who said: "Quit while they still want more!" Too many speakers talk too long. Better to leave out some stories you wanted to tell or other points you wanted to make than to overstay your welcome.

Elaine Fantle Shimberg, TV personality, author of *How to Be a Successful Housewife/Writer*, and co-author of *Coping with Kids on Vacation*.

My advice for beginning speakers is this:

1. Know your audience. The greatest speech in the world falls flat and on deaf ears if it is given to the wrong audience.

2. Know your subject.

3. Speak simply. Don't try to dazzle with your brilliance. The purpose of a speech is to communicate.

4. Always leave them wanting more.

5. Maintain eye contact; the ceiling will be there without your watching it.
6. Relax and have fun.

Evelyn Christenson, president of United Prayer Ministries, and author of *What Happens When Women Pray*, *"Lord, Change Me!"*, and *Gaining Through Losing*.

I feel the most important part of public speaking is making it transferable to one's audience.

Do use real-life examples from your own life or those you know. Then base all points and lessons on Scripture so they are transferable to the listener, not just an ear-tingling or perhaps hair-raising story. These may be entertaining, but basically useless to your audience unless they, too, can use the wisdom, comfort, rebuke, etc., which you found in and applied from the Bible.

Of course, prayer is essential in Christian speech preparation. This will guarantee thoughts from God, not just your pre-conceived ideas. It also will give God a chance to guard you from erroneous thinking; and since He, not you, knows the needs and potential of those in your audience, allows Him to put His thoughts in your mind.

Marlene Lefever, executive editor of Ministry Resources, David C. Cook Publishing Co., and author of *Growing Creative Children* and other books.

Organize what you have to say before you speak. I'm amazed at how many people have a vague idea of where they want to go and what they hope to accomplish, but when it comes to specifics they wing it. People organize in different ways. For some, organization will mean making a point-by-point outline. For others, five words on a card will do the trick. For me, however, a script is best. I think in paragraphs. With a script, I make certain I say everything in the time that I have to say it. Scripting fits my personality and because it is right for me it doesn't kill the life in what I have to communicate. No one organizational method works for everyone, but the advice still stands firm — be organized.

Practice what you have to say aloud. You may even want to tape what you have to say, and check whether your voice is as pleasant as it might be. Often women need to lower their voice just slightly. As I practice aloud, I can work on effective pauses and expression.

Share what you have to say with one objective person. For me, that person is my husband. He's helped tone my speeches by saying things such as, "How many people are going to know that word? Isn't there a better one?" or, "That point gets lost in the illustration. I can't remember what you were talking about before you started your story."

Look at the people you are talking to — not over their heads. Really strive for eye contact. I'll often find as people look back at me whether they are connecting with me. When I feel I'm losing them, I can adjust what I have to say — shorten or throw in another illustration. The best content in the world is no good if the line between the speaker and the listeners is broken.

Memorize your first and last sentences. It adds polish to what you're saying.

Let how you talk express your personality. Work at keeping your voice natural. If you yawn right before you get up to speak — don't let anyone see you — you may be more relaxed for those scary sentences. (I talk a lot with my hands, one on one or in front of a group. My hands help my words come out right; for me that's natural, for other people it may not be.)

Pray about what you're going to say. Have a prayer partner who is praying with you. I want "eye contact" with God as I talk as well as with my audience.

Ruth Stafford Peale, (chief executive officer of Foundation for Christian Living; author of many articles and of *The Adventure of Being a Wife.*

My advice to anyone who wishes to learn the art of public speaking is to train themselves to do this without notes. It is all right to use an outline, but the actual presentation should be spontaneous, enthusiastic, and very practical.

Any speech should include illustrative material. An outline can be divided into two or three sections, but each point should be interestingly illustrated by telling of personal experiences. I find that people will remember stories that I tell far more readily than points I have made in my presentations. But, of course, these stories must illustrate the message being conveyed.

Make your speech short enough that the audience does not tire. Most women go beyond a logical stopping point, and this is a mistake.

Patricia J. Brewer, founder of Blanket of Prayer.

The best piece of advice I could give women who are fearful about getting up to speak before a group would be to somehow obtain a video film of themselves and view it with the idea in mind of seeing the good as well as the bad. I am convinced that it will do wonders for their self-confidence. The most important thing to remember is to keep going back again and again. Fear can be overcome, but it takes more than one or two speeches.

Dr. Vonette Bright, co-founder of Campus Crusade for Christ.

When I asked Dr. Bright what advice she would give beginning speakers, she looked me straight in the eye, and with John the Baptist fervor said, "Tell them to get started!"

Part **5**

Proceed

13

Applause, Applause, Applause

And the Lord said to Paul in the night by a vision, "Do not be afraid any longer, but go on speaking and do not be silent; for I am with you.

Acts 18:9, 10

If your husband called home and said, "Hi, Honey, I'm bringing home five thousand for dinner tonight," how would you respond?

Probably like this: "Five thousand! You've got to be kidding! I only have five loaves of bread and two fish, just enough for the family. We can't feed five thousand! Besides, I don't have that many matching place settings. I'd have to run across town for more fish, and the budget would be shot for the rest of the year!"

Imagine how incredulous the disciples must have looked when Jesus told them to feed the masses (see Matt. 14:15–

21). Yet this is a timeless illustration of what God can do with little.

Carol Kent, originator of *Speak Up With Confidence* believes "the Christian who knows the power of God and is willing to give his/her POTENTIAL to Him, will live in the humble realization that God often allows the person with little natural ability to do His greatest work."[1]

I agree. When you offer your little fish to God, he can make you into a whale of a speaker.

If you have already decided speaking is not your "bag," you decided too soon. It is the same as deciding from the crib you will never master walking, or after trying it once and bumping your head you never try again.

In my years of teaching public speaking, only a handful have voluntarily taken my course. For hundreds of others it was a graduation requirement and they had no choice. Only two students ever claimed not to be afraid: a combat veteran, and a professional speaker who took the course to learn better organizational skills.

Here are some comments from other students after one semester of public speaking:

"I'm leaving with more self-confidence. Thanks."

"I think I look and sound like a confident speaker now and not a basket case."

"I'll never be a great speaker, but I will never again be afraid to get up and try to be a good speaker. Thanks for the confidence."

To God be the glory! I do not hand out confidence in little brown bags at the end of every semester. It comes

1. Carol Kent, *Speak Up with Confidence* (Brochure).

from within each person as an outgrowth of doing the thing they fear the most. The same confidence is waiting patiently within you for its release.

School is out. So now what do you do with all this wonderful knowledge? You begin. Write your testimony even if no one has asked for it. Think like an unbeliever and write answers to questions no one has asked yet. Study Christian women in leadership positions. Start volunteering to make small speaking announcements. Speak up in Sunday school. Listen to as many professional speakers as possible. Take a speech course and learn to talk to real people. Ask God to use you and he will.

Norman Vincent Peale tells us this:

> It is a proven law of human nature that as you imagine yourself to be and as you act on the assumption that you are what you see yourself as being, you will in time strongly tend to become, *provided* you persevere in the process.[2]

Imagine what you could be!

A pastor's wife was in one of my classes. Our friendship outlasted the semester, and we shared much. Once she commented. "I look at you and wish I could do what you do, but I never realized what you went through to get there. I only see the way you are now." I was stunned. I suppose to a student the teacher appears always confident. What she hadn't seen was the years I was unable to hold a conversation about anything more exciting than Big Bird, when having coffee with more than one neighbor at a time was an overwhelming threat, and walking into church was like

2. Norman Vincent Peale, *Enthusiasm Makes the Difference* (New York: Fawcett, 1985), p. 20.

taking the center runway at the Miss America pageant —
after losing.

We sit in the audience and think, "I wish I could do that."
We admire seasoned leaders, not knowing the path that
produced the present result. All speakers start at the bottom; some just start there sooner than others.

Author and international speaker Jill Briscoe explains her
beginnings in the public eye this way:

> I had always wanted to speak and teach. I knew I had
> some talents in these directions, since I had obtained good
> grades in school for speech and drama and enjoyed the
> classroom as a teacher. But how was I to find out if I had
> been spiritually gifted to teach the Scriptures? How could
> I know if God had called me to this ministry? Searching
> the Bible, I began to underline principles that were relevant
> to my questions. I read that all followers of Christ were
> commanded to share their faith, and I must start right
> where I was, teaching what I knew. As I began to articulate
> my faith to my friends and neighbors, I discovered the ones
> and twos I spoke to had relatives and friends they desired
> me to speak to as well. As they brought them to me, it
> became a practical necessity for us all to meet together on
> one night, and so my first Bible class began.[3]

Are you called? Jill Briscoe responds to this question.
"What is a call? It is simply doing the next obvious thing
that needs to be done — and doing it with all we have."[4] For
me, right now, that next thing is the dishes!

For one woman the call came among cafeteria trays. At
a four-day conference, I had spent one afternoon giving

---

3. Jill Briscoe, *Queen of Hearts: The Role of Today's Woman Based on Proverbs 31*
(Old Tappan, N.J.: Revell, 1984), p. 32.
   4. Ibid., p. 33.

Mary speaking pointers. She wasn't sure she would be speaking, but did have some issues with which she was concerned. I suggested she continue to develop her skills by attending Florence Littauer's CLASS seminars. An hour later in the cafeteria, as she put her dinner tray in the rack, there lay a CLASS brochure on the tray of dirty dishes above hers.

A call may not always be so obvious, or it may not come at all. We are not all mouths in the body of Christ, but we are all commanded to share our faith and be ready to answer those who question us about it. I think we can have confidence that the Lord will enable us to accomplish this. As we bring our ones and twos to him there will be joy in heaven (see Luke 15:7), and you can bet the angels will applaud.

> Now then go,
> and I, even I,
> will be with your mouth.
> and teach you what you are to say.
>
> Exod. 4:12

Additional Resources

B eyond this book the Christian woman has available many resources to develop speaking skills. The following list contains organizations and publications geared to assist the speaker in developing her speaking skills.

Clubs and Organizations

National Speakers Association
P.O. Box 29313
Phoenix, AZ 85038
(602) 265-1001

Toastmasters International
World Headquarters
P.O. Box 10400
Santa Ana, CA 92711
(714) 542-6793

International Training in Communication
2519 Woodland Drive
Anaheim, CA 92801
(714) 995-3660

Religious Speech Communication Association
Carolyn Keefe, Ed.D., Executive Secretary
West Chester University
West Chester, PA 19383
(215) 436-2450

Workshops

Christian Leaders and Speakers Seminars (Florence
Littauer)
1666 E. Highland Ave.
San Bernardino, CA 92404
(714) 882-4925
(tapes also available)

Speak Up with Confidence (Carol Kent)
4184 Quaker Hill Dr.
Port Huron, MI 48060
(313) 982-0898

Speaking to Inspire (Nancy Alford)
P.O. Box 413
Roscommon, MI 48653

Books and Publications

Decker Communications Report (monthly)
Decker Communications, Inc.
Yerba Buena West
150 Fourth Street, Suite 200
San Francisco, CA 94103
(415) 546-6100
(workshops also offered)

Plain Public Speaking by Charles R. Grunner

Out of the Salt Shaker and into the World by Rebecca Manley Pippert

Confidence in Public Speaking by Paul Nelson and Judy Pearson

How to Win Friends and Influence People by Dale Carnegie

How to Develop Self-confidence and Influence People by Public Speaking by Dale Carnegie

The Quick and Easy Way to Effective Speaking by Dale Carnegie

Queen of Hearts by Jill Briscoe

Dress and Image Sources

Shades of Beauty by Florence and Marita Littauer
(also available on tape)
Class Book Service
1666 E. Highland Ave.
San Bernardino, CA 92404
(714) 882-4925

The Image of Loveliness by Joanne Wallace

Dress with Style by Joanne Wallace

The Woman's Dress for Success Book by John T. Molloy

Beauty for all Seasons (consultant)
P.O. Box 309
Idaho Falls, ID 83402-0309
(208) 524-4051

Diane Peyton (speaker)
Image Improvement, Inc.
P.O. Box 7679
Salem, OR 97304
(503) 393-2051

Emily Lite (consultant/speaker)
9450 Royal Lane, #3033
Dallas, TX 75243
(214) 340-8172

Bibliography

Baker, Sheridan. *The Practical Stylist*. New York: Crowell, 1962.

Berko, Roy M., Andrew W. Wolvin, and Darlyn R. Wolvin. *Communicating: A Social and Career Focus*. Boston, 1985.

Bowling, Evelyn B. *Voice Power*. Harrisburg, Pa.: Stackpole, 1980.

Braude, Jacob M. *Complete Speaker's and Toastmaster's Library: Speech Openers and Closers*. Englewood Cliffs, N.J.: Prentice-Hall, 1965.

Briscoe, Jill. *Queen of Hearts: The Role of Today's Woman Based on Proverbs 31*. Old Tappan, N.J.: Revell, 1984.

Brown, Charles T., and Charles Van Riper. *Speech and Man*. Englewood Cliffs, N.J.: Prentice-Hall, 1966.

Brown, Joan W. *No Longer Alone*. Old Tappan, N.J.: Revell, 1975.

Carnegie, Dale. *How to Develop Self-Confidence and Influence People by Public Speaking*. New York: Pocket Books, 1956.

————— . *How to Win Friends and Influence People*. New York: Pocket Books, 1964.

————— . *The Quick and Easy Way to Effective Speaking*. New York: Association Press, 1962.

Christenson, Evelyn. *Lord, Change Me!* Wheaton, Ill.: Victor Books, 1977.

191

Deen, Edith. *All the Women of the Bible*. New York: Harper and Row, 1955.

Dobson, James. *Emotions: Can You Trust Them?* Ventura, Calif.: Regal, 1980.

Edwards, Charlotte. *Writing from the Inside Out*. Cincinnati: Writers Digest, 1984.

Fast, Julius. *Body Language*. New York: Evans, 1970.

Gossett, Don. *How to Conquer Fear*. Springdale, Pa.: Whitaker House, 1981.

Gruner, Charles R. *Plain Public Speaking*. New York: Macmillan, 1983.

Kelley, Joseph J. *Speechwriting: The Master Touch*. Harrisburg, Pa.: Stackpole, 1980.

Kunhardt, Philip B. "Abe Lincoln's Failure." *Reader's Digest* (November 1983):191–200.

Littauer, Florence. *Christian Leaders and Speakers Seminars*. Eugene, Oreg. 1983. Audio cassettes.

————. *It Takes So Little to Be Above Average*. Eugene, Oreg.: Harvest House, 1983.

Lucas, Stephen E. *The Art of Public Speaking*. New York: Random, 1983.

Lustberg, Arch. *Testifying with Impact*. Washington, D.C.: U.S. Chamber of Commerce, 1982.

————. *Winning at Confrontation*. Washington, D.C.: U.S. Chamber of Commerce, 1984.

Mainprize, Don. *Enjoy the Christian Life*. Wheaton, Ill.: Tyndale, 1966.

Minnick, Wayne C. *Public Speaking*. 2d ed. Boston: Houghton Mifflin.

Molloy, John T. *Dress for Success*. New York: Warner Books, 1975.

————. *The Woman's Dress for Success Book*. New York: Warner Books, 1977.

Nelson, Paul E., and Judy C. Pearson. *Confidence in Public Speaking*. 2d ed. Dubuque, Iowa: William C. Brown, 1984.

Ochs, Donovan J., and Anthony C. Winkler. *A Brief Introduction to Speech*. New York: Harcourt Brace Jovanovich, 1983.

Palms, Roger. *Living under the Smile of God*. Wheaton, Ill.: Tyndale, 1984.

Peale, Norman Vincent. *Enthusiasm Makes the Difference*. New York: Fawcett, 1978.

————. *You Can Have God's Help with Daily Problems*. New York, 1980.

Pippert, Rebecca M. *Out of the Saltshaker and into the World.* Downers Grove, Ill.: Inter-Varsity, 1979.

Rankin, Peg. *Glorify God and Enjoy Him Forever.* Ventura, Calif.: Regal, 1981.

Swindoll, Charles. "Why Are Some Preachers Better Than Others?" *The Christian Herald* (July/August 1984):20–22.

Wallace, Joanne. *Dress with Style.* Old Tappan, N.J.: Revell, 1983.

——————. *The Image of Loveliness.* Old Tappan, N.J.: Revell, 1978.